JOURNEY TO THE FATHER'S HEART

ONE WOMAN'S JOURNEY TO KNOW THE TRUE, UNCONDITIONAL LOVE OF THE FATHER

WENDI REES

ISBN (paperback): 978-1-64184-942-5

ISBN (ebook): 978-1-64184-943-2

TABLE OF CONTENTS

PART THREE
THE MINISTRY AND THE MESSAGE

To my husband, Jim: Without you, this journey would have been impossible. God has used you in such a dynamic way in my life to help me see and understand so many things. Just as I read to you, on our wedding day, the letter I wrote explaining how I waited for my "knight in shining armor," you are still that same hero to me today. You've endured so much more than I know you bargained for when you married me. Yet, just like Jesus, you've never left nor forsaken me, although you've had plenty of reasons to! I love you with all that I am!

To My Beloved Children, Jace, Jaxon, Jenna and Jessa: How much I wish you knew the depth of the love I feel for you. Each of you are a gift from God, and there is not enough time left in my life to thank Him for giving each of you to me. Thank you for loving me and patiently walking through life with me. I know I have not been a perfect momma to you, but each of you know without a doubt that I love you up to the moon, as big as the sky, and with all my heart. I pray that each of you walk with the Lord every day of your lives and remember that He will never leave or forsake you no matter what. He is our ultimate perfect example of a parent that I long to be to each of you!

There is nothing more magnificent than the heavenly
Father's love.

This love sees us as we are and with no pretense, lavishes us
with unlimited acceptance and belonging.

His arms are always open wide, ready for the moment we turn
and run into them.

When we turn to Him, He doesn't require a deep plea
or a long story,
He says: "Come, you belong to Me, I will never leave you
or forsake you."

He takes no account of our condition nor will He use
our condition as a barrier… *only an invitation.*

The moment we cry out to Him, He hears us, and He is there.

INTRODUCTION

GOD WILL GIVE US BEAUTY FOR ASHES

Can you remember the end of an amazing campfire with friends or family where you laughed, ate s'mores and made cherished memories? After the songs are over and the last square of Hershey's chocolate gobbled up, everyone goes home, and all that's left from the fire are the charred black-gray ashes. Those ashes are usually thrown out and forgotten. They are the "left-overs" from the experience that preceded it. That's what happens to ashes; they are not good for much except when they come from the burned out and charred experiences of our lives.

When I look back at my life before it was touched by Christ, it seemed like there was nothing but a trail of hurt, abuse, loss, disappointment, rejection, loneliness, and ashes. Ashes from our lives should be thrown out and forgotten, right?

No, that's not right. It's a lie from the enemy. The lie he tries relentlessly to make us believe that we are damaged and worthless and should be thrown out and forgotten.

It's not true. God has a remarkable way of taking our ashes and turning them into something of value, beyond anything we could have asked or imagined. Ashes are no match for the goodness of God. In fact, He delights in making beauty out of crumbled up, unworthy, invaluable things and He does it in all kinds of ways. Isaiah 61:3 says that He gives us "a crown of beauty, oil of joy and garments of praise, instead of our ashes, our mourning, and our heaviness."

When you and I see useless ashes, He sees an invitation to give you:

A crown of beauty.
Oil of joy.
Garments of praise.

Doesn't that amaze you? It amazes me every single day. Instead of our ashes, we get a crown of beauty to wear as we hold our heads up in His presence, we get precious oil that makes us joyful and a garment of praise in place of the spirit of heaviness. What's more important than this is that we get to be in relationship with God who deeply loves us. He doesn't give us what we deserve or what other people tell us we deserve; He gives us gifts of mercy.

From my ashes, He created an unshakeable hope in me. Hope is the expectation of and the desire for good. Hope in God saved my life and gave me something to hold on to in my darkest hours. I wish I could tell you that my darkest hours didn't involve my family or people that I loved. I would also like to tell you that my darkest hours didn't involve what I learned in church or that they didn't confuse my view of God and His love for me. If I told you those things they would not be true, they would only be wishes. My life was impacted with darkness much too early and much too deeply. Every child wants a happy childhood, to grow up in a loving family. I was no different. However, in my family things that should have been right were not right and parents who should have protected me from harm were responsible for bringing tremendous harm into my life. If it were not for the saving grace of God, I would have been lost in depression and despair. I didn't know my worth or my value. Was I a child to be cherished and treasured or one to be used and discarded? I didn't know.

But God knew.

My prayer is that this book will remind you of who you are and of who God is for you no matter where you've come from. As you read, think of me sitting with you in a circle of close friends sharing my story. I am a friend who has listened to many, many women tell their stories. Some of the women are past the most hurtful parts of their journey and walking with God through the healing process. Others are in their darkest hours searching for the light ahead of them. Wherever you are, I hope you can feel the gentle touch of God's love and the support of a caring friend. Knowing you are not alone in your struggle is the first step in disarming the plan of the enemy. He wants to isolate you in your pain, play with your mind and feed you lies until you completely give up! I've heard deeply saddening stories of young girls who have taken their own lives because they were desperate to find relief from the prison of shame they built for themselves. This is not God's plan, it's the enemy's plan to remove all hope of the redemption God has planned for you on the other side of your pain.

I'm not the authority on hurt or brokenness. I've included quotes and expert research from people who are authorities in those areas.

I not only share my story but my journey. The curtain of my heart is pulled back to let you know what was going on inside. There are entries that I wrote in my journal and personal letters.

I share Scriptures that I hope will encourage you in your journey to the Father's heart of love, and at the end of each section, I offer a prayer to God for His true love toward His daughters and sons.

Redemption and healing are yours. It's a gift of love waiting for you to reach out and receive it.

PART ONE

DECEIT, DECEPTION, AND DEVASTATION

HER DESPERATION LED HER
TO JESUS

D o you know the story of the woman who had been bleeding for twelve years? She exhausted her resources, hope, and energy going from doctor to doctor searching for healing.

I had read the passage of the woman with the issue of blood many times in the Bible (Mark 5:22-34) but it wasn't until my friend Chris helped me take a closer look that my eyes and heart opened to the depth of God's love displayed in those Scriptures. Here's what he shared with me:

THE WOMAN WITH THE ISSUE OF BLOOD

One day Jesus was walking by Capernaum, near the Sea of Galilee, when an official of the synagogue, Jairus, stopped Him and begged for His help. He told him that his little daughter had just died, but that he knew she would live if He would come and put His hands on her. Jesus had become well known in this region because of the miracles He performed. He was always thronged by crowds who followed Him everywhere. They pressed in, longing to get a closer look at what He was doing and saying. Many just wanted to be near Him.

The Scripture is clear that this man was seeking help for his *"little daughter"*—not an adult child. His little daughter who hadn't even had a chance to become a woman yet.

He specifically asks Jesus to "lay hands on her"—to touch his little girl and make her well so she can live. Jesus followed the man as he led the way to his daughter.

As they walked they met one of the most pitiful characters of the gospels. She is introduced as "a woman who had a discharge of blood for twelve years."

This meant that at some point, she started her menstrual cycle, and it had never stopped. In our day, that would be terribly inconvenient. In her day, it was devastating.

The Levitical (Leviticus 15:19-33) laws prescribed that a woman was ceremonially unclean during the seven days of her menstrual cycle. Anyone who touched her or any surface she sat or lied on was also unclean.

Keep in mind that the original intent of "unclean" did not connect to sin or moral impurity – far from it. Ceremonial uncleanness was a way of setting something apart from other things. In the Jewish world, blood was considered the very element of life. Life was in the blood. Bleeding was taken seriously.

The woman was not only facing the consequences of losing blood, but she also suffered the restrictions with being ceremonially unclean. Most likely, she couldn't handle money, tools, food, or anything else necessary for daily living because, like her, those things would become unclean.

Consider the implication. For most women of child-bearing years, a menstrual cycle lasted seven days. Seven days that she was not able to perform her normal duties.

Some say that many Jewish communities had a tent just outside of the village where women stayed for seven days during their cycle. Consider the relationship building that happened as the girls and women from their early teens to menopause gathered in overlapping seven days. It was a beautiful system of one generation connecting, sharing, and learning from the other.

As well as the system worked most of the time, sometimes it broke down. It had broken in the case of the woman who could not stop bleeding. She went to the tent like every other woman to wait out her seven days…but after seven days, she was still bleeding.

After 14, 21, 28…*still bleeding.*

In the tent, the other women came and went. They experienced the normal celebrations of life; Marriage, childbirth and so on. But not this woman, all she had was blood. Blood that made her an outcast.

She went from doctor to doctor without success. They were unable to help, and she was out of money to keep paying them. The Bible says she "suffered much" at the hands of the doctors.

Her family isn't mentioned in the passage, but I wonder, where was her father? Why wasn't he out seeking the Healer for his daughter? Had they abandoned her?

Likely, her malady was interpreted as a sign of God's dissatisfaction with her or as a punishment.

Alone, abused, unwanted, unclean, unloved, and untouchable—she was a ghost in her own community. She was severely judged, seen as insufficient and flawed. Are there any worse feelings for a woman?

With all of this, she heard that Jesus the Healer was coming. She knew of His miracles and how He changed lives. She desperately wanted her life changed; she wanted to be healed.

But she had a problem.

When Jesus healed people, He *touched* them, and she could not be touched.

If He touched her, she would make Him unclean. Then He couldn't heal anyone else for a while. Plus, she assumed there was no way that He would allow Himself to be touched.

Jesus, walking with a Synagogue official well versed in the details of the law, and almost swallowed up by the crowd, was passing by.

She decided on a desperate strategy of sneaking up through the crowd. This time she needed to go unnoticed, she needed to be invisible. When Jesus came by she would get close enough to reach and touch just the tip of His garment. She believed that's all it would take.

Would this make Him unclean? Maybe it should, but no one would even know she touched Him.

Would she be healed?

Surely, she would; she had faith that His healing power would not fail her.

Jesus passed by. She did it—she touched Him, and *she was healed.*

Immediately, the bleeding stopped. She knew it. Before she could celebrate, she heard the words she was used to hearing.

"Who touched me?"

The disciples were clueless. They tried to explain to Jesus that the crowd was all around Him, anyone could have touched Him. They tried to move Him along. He ignored them. He knew that power left Him. He was searching the crowd.

She saw Him looking. Should she scramble back or try to hide? What will happen if the crowd and the synagogue official found out what she did? It would be hard for her to hide or escape when she was down on her hands and knees.

Then He saw her.

The crowd parted as He moved toward her.

Afraid, trembling, she went to Him. She couldn't hold it in one minute longer. The whole story flooded out of her while everyone stood and watched.

When her story was done spilling out, I think she finally met His eyes as they gazed upon her with tenderness and love. Jesus spoke two words.

Most people think Jesus' first words were "your faith has made you whole."

But that isn't correct. Before He spoke those words, He said something much more powerful, something that would alter her to the very core.

His first words were *"My daughter."*

He called her "daughter." Before he did anything, He let the crowd know that He claimed her. Take a moment to think of how this must have felt to her. She'd been called many names, none of them as honoring as what she'd just heard. Being called daughter gave her a place to belong and Someone to belong to. He didn't do it in secret; He did it openly for all those watching to see. At that moment, her prior shame must have turned into rejoicing.

This is the only person Jesus called "daughter" in all four gospels. When she had nothing to offer Him, *He claimed her as His*. Before the official could get angry or quote Leviticus, Jesus made it clear that *He claimed her*. Who would dare speak back to that?

Jesus encouraged her to "go" in her newfound freedom. Even if they never saw each other again, she knew her life had meaning and purpose and that she belonged. God incarnate spoke into her identity to let her know that she was *His daughter*. *Then* He said, "Your faith has made you well; go in peace, and be healed of your disease."

When we bring uncleanness to Jesus, we don't stain Him; it's His purity that cleanses us. No one is unwanted, not even one. Jesus and Jairus continued walking. When they reached the home of Jairus, another daughter is healed, brought back to life by the love of Jesus.

HER STORY MY STORY

I cried when Chris first told me this story, and I've cried many times since then at the retelling of it. At first, I cried for the woman. Then I cried for myself. The woman had a situation that brought her shame and made her an outcast. It took away her identity and caused those around her to misunderstand who she really was. They labeled her, and I'm sure she labeled herself. Before meeting Jesus, she did all she could do on her own to acquire her healing. She tried until she ran out of resources.

She used what little hope she had left to reach out and touch the hem of the garment of One she'd heard might heal her as He passed by.

Jesus was on His way to a completely different destination when she got His attention with just one touch. She reached out for her body to be healed, for the blood to stop flowing. However, He knew she longed for something deeper than that.

He knew she longed for belonging, to no longer be an outcast.

First, He gave her identity, *then* He spoke of her healing. Before Jesus said anything, He called her daughter. To me this is a perfect act of love—to be called *"daughter."* In an open display, He made His priority clear to her and everyone around her. Things had changed for this woman. She wasn't the same woman they knew before. Now she would be known as the one Jesus called "daughter." They would also know her as the woman who used to bleed but after meeting Jesus was healed.

God showed up to give her not only what she needed but what she wanted the most. It's the same in our lives. When God touches us, He wants first to establish our identity and clearly define our belonging and, at the same moment, bring healing to our broken places.

No matter how we see ourselves, He sees us as "daughter" or "son" and openly claims us as His own.

I AM MY FATHER'S DAUGHTER

When I was fourteen, I was kicked out of my home by the one that I loved most in the world, my father. He and my mom had recently divorced, and things weren't going so well with me and my soon-to-be step-mom. I felt lost and disillusioned. I was confused and didn't understand how he could send me away and go on with his life. I wondered what I did wrong to be treated this way. I thought that if my dad had to choose between me and anyone else, he would surely choose me. After all, I was his daughter; I belonged to him.

The day he came to my school and told me he was putting me on a plane and sending me away from the family, I was in shock. I didn't want to believe it was true, but it was. That evening I was on a plane leaving my home and my brothers and sister behind. I felt like an outcast from my family, like I had been thrown out with the trash.

As a little girl, I admired my dad more than anyone. He was the smartest person I knew. To me, he was the king of the world. He hung the moon and could make the stars twinkle. Other kids had nice parents but none of them had my daddy.

He was an Independent Fundamental Baptist preacher with extraordinary charisma and influence in our community. If an outsider came to my town and asked anyone at the gas station or the grocery store if they knew my dad, the answer would be, "Oh yes, we know him." People knew him because they went to our church or because they'd met him around town and remembered his ease of connecting with them in a way that made them feel special.

Dad was the picture of perfection. Things seemed to always go right for him. He started pastoring our church and then started the school that we went to. He was a busy man with big visions for the church and his ministry. I loved him and wanted to be with him every chance I got even when he was doing church work. It was the most natural thing for me to tag along with him when he was called to do hospital visits or to visit a family in need.

At the end of each church service, someone closed in prayer. While all heads were bowed and eyes closed, my dad would leave the pulpit and walk to the front doors of the church to personally shake hands with congregation members as they left the sanctuary. I hardly let a service go by that I didn't leap out of my seat and walk proudly down the aisle with him and stand by his side at the doors. Sometimes, I stayed until the last person left the building. I was as proud as I could be to be his daughter.

The best thing about being my dad's daughter was getting to go on daddy-daughter dates once a month. It was just the two of us. He would show up at the school early and take me out for the rest of the day. I got to pick where we went. Sometimes we went to eat or to the mall.

On those days, I could hardly concentrate on my school work. My heart would beat fast with joy and delight as I thought, *My daddy is coming for me!* There was nothing better than that.

I felt safe and free from harm when I was walking in my dad's shadow.

I wasn't the only one who thought he hung the moon. The people in our church and community felt the same way. He had a type of star quality and charm, and he was admired by everyone around us. They not only loved him, but in their own way, they worshipped him. It was common for me to hear the members telling him how much they admired him. He had a gift for making them feel better about their often-stressful lives.

He connected and bonded with others with such depth that they just wanted to follow him. The congregants learned to obey and treat him with unquestioned respect. He commanded loyalty, and those around him were more than willing to comply. The church was his life. That's where we spent most of our time. Many of the memories from my early childhood were of things that happened at the church. He taught our congregation his idea of what it meant to be devoted in our faith. We thought that we were being taught to be devoted to God and His ways when we were really being taught to be devoted to my dad and *his* ways.

My siblings and I lived under the watchful eyes of the church community. My dad used to tell the congregation that if they saw any of his kids misbehaving when he was not around, to feel free to correct us and tell him about it later. You can imagine, we didn't get away with anything. Being perfect was my goal. I thought that if my dad demanded perfection, God was the very same way.

What I didn't know is that God gives pure, unconditional love. I didn't do anything to earn it or deserve it. His love is a gift.

1 John 4:7 says:

Beloved, let us love one another, for love is from God, and whoever loves has been born of God and knows God. And, 1 Corinthians 13:4-8 says: *Love is patient, love is kind; love does not envy or boast; it is not arrogant or rude. It does not insist on its own way; it is not irritable or resentful. It does not rejoice at wrongdoing but rejoices with the truth. Love bears all things, believes all things, hopes all things, endures all things. Love never ends. ESV*

The way my dad brought us up caused me a lot of confusion about God. I knew that God could read my mind and at any given time He could strike me dead if He wished. I didn't know Him as a warm and loving Father. I certainly didn't think He loved me with an everlasting love. No, I pretty much thought that God's love was tentative, easily angered, poised and ready to punish me if I did anything wrong. If I was good, He loved me; if I was not good, He was angry with me and would abandon me.

I didn't know that this was not a realistic representation of God's love. God's love is not pretend or counterfeit. It's honorable; it's the real thing. In fact, there is no real love outside of God's love. I was taught that I needed to be perfect so that God could accept me and love me, I tried as hard as I could until my journey to the heart of the Father taught me differently. There are times when I still fight the need to be perfect even though I know that I will never be perfect and that I am always growing, changing and moving from glory to glory. His love is not like a roller coaster that goes up and down depending on my performance or behavior. Before I ever knew Him, He loved me, I didn't do anything to earn it.

I learned a lot about Scriptures, the Bible, and the rules. We learned about religion which had more to do with what things looked like on the outside instead of the condition of our hearts on the inside. We learned to do what we were told. Unfortunately, this is the case with many people in the church. They learn about religion and about keeping rules but not about the powerful, strong love of God that can save our souls and make all things new in His time.

2 Corinthians 5:17 says:

Therefore, if anyone is in Christ, he is a new creation. The old has passed away, behold the new has come. ESV

My dad was trying to get us to become "new" when we were already new because of Christ and what He did for us on the cross. Church activities were the core of my dad's life. He was competitive and made it his goal to have the biggest congregation in town. If people didn't come to the church on their own, we had a bus ministry that would pick them up. Dad would drive one of the buses and our bus director, who I called grandpa, would drive another. They'd have contests, and whoever brought in the most people won. The loser had to do crazy things like ride a donkey backward in the rain in the parking lot of the church or eat a chocolate-covered cricket. There were plenty of fun and games on the outside, but my dad had other things hidden in the background of his life that were not in keeping with his mission as a pastor. He had a set of standards for himself and another for everyone else. My dad, like many Independent Fundamental Baptist (see Appendix A) preachers, believed that he only answered to God for his actions, which meant that he could pretty much do whatever he wanted to do. If someone tried to say anything different, they were forced out of the church.

There was no such thing as being a part of my dad's world if you were not going to be committed to him and his way of doing things (see Appendix B). Church members who were not even involved in any formal ministry felt they had to ask for permission to do normal things like go on vacation or miss a Sunday service. My dad was determined to enforce his rules. It was easier to do what he said rather than question him and suffer his disapproval. Many of the rules were not spiritual but centered around his control and demand for loyalty. To us, this meant that true Christian people didn't do things that looked bad or suggest there was any bad thing in us. This kind of leadership causes religious pressure that often leads to spiritual abuse (see Appendix C) of congregation and family members.

We would not have thought that what we were living under was spiritual abuse, but we knew it was certainly control. Girls couldn't wear pants or shirts with writing on them. We had to be careful not to draw attention to our bodies. We couldn't swim in the pool with boys. We couldn't go to movies or listen to any music other than church music. We couldn't read magazines or books other than the Bible and our school books. Doing any of these things would lead us to Hell. We read through the Bible, memorized Scripture, and were careful to be obedient to stay in the good graces of the Lord. I read the Bible and wondered why

I couldn't find my dad's rules. When I asked him about it, he would say to do the rules because he said to do them. Then he shut my questioning down. Eventually, I stopped asking.

The list of the things we couldn't do was long and impossible for anybody to keep. Apparently, it was impossible for him as well because much of what he told us not to do he did in secrecy. I had no idea what was going on in his world outside of church. Looking back, I'm reminded that the Bible says in I Samuel 16:7, "Man looks at the outer appearance, but God looks at the heart." The things he struggled with were hidden below the surface and impacted my life and the lives of our family and our church. When everything eventually came out, we were surprised, but it wasn't a surprise to God.

My dad was well known and had authority, but he also had pride that led to his downfall. Like King Uzziah in 2 Chronicles.

2 Chronicles 26:15-16.

"His fame spread far and wide, for he was greatly helped until he became powerful. But after Uzziah became powerful, his pride led to his downfall. He was unfaithful to the Lord his God." ESV

When a leader is unfaithful to God, he becomes an instrument of pain to those around him. Every person needs the grace of God to help them walk in truth and in faith. No matter how spiritual pastors or leaders may seem, they are never above the temptation of the flesh and will always need the grace of God to do the work that He has called them to do.

CHURCH ON SUNDAY TO GET TO HEAVEN

We went to church every Sunday. I believed that you had to go to church on Sunday if you wanted to go to Heaven. Many Sunday mornings, as we drove off to church, I saw my neighbors' cars in their driveways and wondered why they didn't go to church like we did. Didn't they love God? Didn't they know that you can't go to Heaven if you stayed home on Sunday? I felt sad for my neighbors and would often go to their homes and invite them to church, or I would get my dad to invite them. I wanted them to know and love Jesus. It troubled me when I saw them do things like listen to rock music or drink alcohol.

One day, I saw a neighbor boy drinking a beer in his backyard. There were no fences separating our yards, so I could see everything that was going on. If he kept drinking that beer, he would be lost and separated from God. I wanted to save him. When his back was turned, I ran as fast as I could across the lawn into his yard and poured out his beer. I wanted to do my part in helping people go to Heaven. I went door to door and invited kids to Sunday school. I rode the bus with my dad to pick people up. I wanted people to know Jesus, even though I didn't fully understand what that meant.

I was working my way to Heaven by doing the things a good church girl (especially a preacher's daughter) would do.

REALITY CHANGED

My mom and dad seemed to get along well enough most of the time, but then I noticed something change between them. When I was young, they had fights and disagreements that they tried to hide from us, but we knew something was going on. We didn't know why they were mad at each other or who started it; we just knew things were not right.

I asked my mom if they were getting a divorce. She looked at me with surprise and asked me why I asked her such a thing. I told her that I knew other kids whose parents were getting divorced, and I wanted to know if we were going to be like them. She told me that I didn't have anything to worry about and that I shouldn't think about it.

Dad spent more time at the church than he did at home. I could see them pulling apart and hoped it was just my imagination. I thought the arguments may have been my mom's fault; maybe she was doing something to make dad angry. I had so little knowledge of what was going on with my parents.

Because of their continued fighting, mom would often travel to Florida where her parents lived. When she was away, each of us kids would take turns sleeping in the "big bed" with dad. This went on for years and years. On one of those trips, it was

JOURNEY TO THE FATHER'S HEART

my turn in the big bed. and I was so excited. I did what I would normally do—I got in the bed and went to sleep.

I was awakened by something that would change my world forever. I could feel my dad touching me in ways that a father should never touch his daughter. I was a young girl, only eleven years old. I didn't know anything about what was happening to me. I knew it wasn't right, but it was my dad. He's the one who taught us the rules and would tell us that we shouldn't do such things, but here he was doing things to me. I tried to make sense of it, but what my dad started that night never made sense to me. It happened more than once. When my mom was away, or any chance when he was alone with me, he abused me. I felt like I should tell someone. He said if I told, my mom would leave, and it would tear our family apart and all of it would be my fault. The night he started touching me broke my heart right along with my body.

The abuse that started that night continued until I was sent away from home at fourteen.

My father, my hero, was no longer a safe person in my life. I didn't know the word *molestation*. I didn't even know what sex was. For years, I kept quiet because I didn't want to break my family apart and be like the other kids I knew whose parents got divorced. I thought it was my job to keep it all together. One time while I was on a mission trip, one of the kids told me they saw my dad and another woman doing flirtatious things under the table. I thought I was going to smack them because they were talking bad about my dad. Even with everything he was doing to me, I loved him unconditionally and was completely loyal to him.

I never said a word about what was going on. My parents continued to fight. The morning of December 30, my dad woke us all up and said to meet in the family room for a family pow-wow. We'd had many of these pow-wows in my lifetime, but this one would change everything. With all four kids lined up side-by-side on the couch, my dad sitting on the coffee table, and my mom in the white rocking chair, we heard the news that in the next four days we would be leaving our home. We were told that on

January 1, my dad would resign from the church and that on the 3rd we would be driving to Texas where we would be starting another church. Mom was going to be going to her parents' house during the transition and would meet us in Texas in just a couple of weeks. The move was going to be hard on her, so they decided that she would leave for Florida while dad drove with us kids to Texas and the deacons would pack our house up and get our belongings to Texas. The truth was that my parents were getting divorced, and I would not be seeing my mom again. I just knew it was all my fault.

Another couple in our church, who had been good friends of our family, were also divorcing. My mom and dad spent a lot of time with them; they even went on a vacation together. After my parents' divorce and the other couple divorced, my mom married the other man, and my dad married the other woman. They just swapped partners. I had a new stepmom and a new stepdad. Everything happened so quickly. Mom was gone. My dad, myself, and my brothers and sister had moved to Texas. My world had suddenly changed. The church and the people I had spent most of my life with were no longer there. I felt alone.

My dad's abuse continued when we got to Texas. I didn't get along with my soon-to-be step-mom who at one time was a trusted friend. We had a big knock-down drag-out fight one night, and right in front of me she told my father that he had to choose; it was her or me. I thought, *Oh well, I'm his firstborn so bye-bye. I'll see you later!* I knew it wasn't much of a choice for him; she would have to leave because I was staying with my dad and my family no matter what.

The next day I went to school as usual. I had just made the cheerleading team. We were having a bake sale, and as I was stirring the nacho cheese, I looked up and saw my dad walking down the hallway. I felt like I did when he would come to pick me up for our father-daughter dates when I was younger. I ran to him to give him a hug. He wasn't happy to see me. My heart sank to the pit of my stomach. I searched his face looking for the twinkle he used to have in his eyes when he picked me up for a day out. It wasn't there. I hugged him, but he didn't hug me back. It was very awkward, and I felt the sting of rejection. My dad didn't choose me. He chose the other woman. He pulled out a plane ticket from his coat pocket and said, "You're going to live with your mom, and you're leaving tonight." Was my dad really letting go of me? New wife, new life, and eventually new kids; "good-bye Wendi." I felt like he was throwing me out with the trash.

That rejection wounded me to my core. As a result, rejection is something I still struggle with to this day. It's not obvious to most people because I've learned to keep it together on the outside, but I can't hide it from my husband or God. In regards to the sexual abuse, there's only one person on the planet, my wonderful husband Jim, who has to deal with anything related to that, but everyone else in my life has to deal with my issues stemming from my dad's rejection.

My dad turned my whole family against me when he put me on that plane and sent me to live with my mother. I'd been loyal and did everything I was supposed to do at church and at home. I was the one who had always been there; the other woman was new. Why wasn't she the one leaving? There were no answers, and the decision had been made. I was being sent away to live with my mom.

My dad had told us that my mom ran off with the other man and didn't want us kids, so I wondered why he was sending me back to someone who didn't want me. Plus, I knew she must hate me because of what happened between my dad and me. After all, that was obviously what made her leave our family and run off with the other man. It was exactly what my dad said would happen if she found out about it, but I never told anyone. How did she know then? I was afraid of how she felt about me.

It took a while to get used to being with my mom because we were never close. We hadn't spent much time together before the divorce, and now I was living with her full-time without the buffer of my dad or brothers or sister. I had to learn how to have a relationship with her. It was weird seeing her married to my high school teacher and softball coach.

I thought my mom knew about the abuse that happened with my dad and that was why she left. But, I soon discovered, she didn't know. After all, my dad told me she would leave if she found out about us, and I had no intention of stirring things up by telling her. It was on a ride home from church when a friend told me something about my dad and the other woman that I couldn't keep to myself. While my dad was still married to my mom, the other woman got pregnant with *his* baby. That pregnancy resulted in a miscarriage. I was furious and went right in to tell my mom. When I told her, she was angry and couldn't believe that I would believe such a thing about my dad. Surely, he would *never* do something like that! I was confused as to why she would think he wouldn't do that after what he did to me. That's when I realized that my mom really had no idea about what had happened with my dad. I ran to my room and slammed the door, realizing that I had backed myself into a corner. Assuming she knew what he had done to me, it only made sense that she would understand why I might believe that my dad was capable of getting the other woman pregnant while still married to my mom. But, at that exact moment, I realized she really didn't know. She had no idea what he had done to me. That meant she didn't leave because of me. It was not my fault that our family split apart.

She banged on my door and demanded that I open it immediately. I wanted desperately to protect her from what she was about to hear because she had no idea what was about to hit her. I had no choice, and I struggled to get the words out. She knew there was something awful that I was keeping from her. With tears streaming down my face, I began to tell my mom what my dad had done to me. The more she heard, the angrier she became. Surprisingly, her anger was completely toward my dad and not at me in the least. It was so different from what I had believed for the past several months. In fact, she told me it was the one good thing that had come from her leaving my dad—he could no longer hurt me.

After I told her the whole story, her anger was obvious, and she wanted to report him to the authorities. I didn't want him to be arrested, so I told her not to call anyone and that I wouldn't talk if she did. There had already been enough trouble for me with my family; I didn't want to cause any more. I kept silent, but on the inside I was dealing with my hurt and pain the best way I could.

My mom lived in the community that we left when we moved to Texas, so I was back with many of my old friends. Everyone had questions and wanted information about why we left and about my parents, especially my dad. When my dad left, the church split. Some people in the community still loved him, but some hated him, which made me very uncomfortable.

After a couple of years of living with my mom and her new husband, the sexual abuse started all over again with him. I couldn't believe it. This was the second husband she'd married that molested me. He had seen how difficult my life had been the past couple of years and the things that I struggled with—eating disorders, depression, anger, and isolation. And now he is abusing me? This time, I didn't keep quiet and went straight to my mom. She wasted no time confronting him, and it immediately stopped. But she was not able to protect me from being abused by other men at school and at church—my eighth-grade homeroom teacher, a Sunday School teacher's husband, a cheerleading sponsor's older brother—the list goes on. I started to wonder if I had a giant sign on my forehead telling men that I was asking for it.

I started acting out at school and was perceived as a "rebellious problem child." This made it even harder to consider telling anyone what was happening to me. I mean, really—who would believe me over these men? They all had some kind of authoritative role in my life. No one would believe the rebellious teenager over the well-respected teacher. The enemy was having a field day in my mind!

By the time I was eighteen years old, I felt like I was a piece of meat, and I was angry. I'd been abused by both of my father figures and so many other men. I thought that sexual pleasure was all I was good for.

I was numb, and I hated anyone in authority. I'd learned that men in authority used their position to get things out of me and to keep me quiet. I started rebelling against all those "rules" that were supposed to make God love me and keep me safe. I didn't need to keep them anymore. What good did it do to keep rules and get hurt and abandoned anyway?

THE DOOR OF DARKNESS

I finished high school and was at a loss for what to do with my life. I started dating a guy I thought I wanted to marry. His sister was dancing at a topless bar, and one day when I was at a tanning salon, I was approached by someone asking me if I wanted a job dancing. I told my boyfriend about it, thinking he would be upset, but to my surprise, he encouraged me to do it. I was so afraid of rejection and disappointing him that I said yes even though I never thought I would do anything like that, especially since I was taught that dancing would send me straight to hell. I was done following rules and decided to go a different way, I was going to dance. I got the job, and my boyfriend drove me to Shotgun Willy's. When we got there, I got out of the car and opened the door to the darkest part of my life.

The dancing world was unlike anything I ever knew existed. Some girls had been there for over fifteen years. I was surrounded by everything I'd always been taught was pure evil. Rock music, immorality, alcohol, and drugs. Everything that was prohibited in my life was now right in my face. It was strange that I would become a dancer when I never danced in my life. I didn't even know how to dance!

When I first started, I was terrified, but after a while, I didn't think about it. When my shift started, I just tuned everything out and danced.

There were things happening around me that I'd never seen before. Girls who danced at the clubs usually abused alcohol and drugs. I didn't touch either. Even though I had gone away from God, I was not willing to throw out all that I'd learned about what might send me to Hell. When I danced, I never had a drop of alcohol, puffed one cigarette, or took drugs. Even though my moral compass was completely messed up, I was too afraid of the wrath of God and what would happen to me if I even got close to alcohol or drugs.

When I danced, in a strange way, I felt safe and protected. For the first time in my life, men could look at me, but they could not touch me. I was gaining control over my own body. I felt like I was safer on the stage than I was in my own home because "Bubba" the bouncer protected us and would pull any man out by their hair if they even tried to touch us. Even though I didn't use drugs or drinking to get high, I was high on the feeling that for the first time there was someone to protect me. If a man tried to touch me, someone would forcibly step in between me and them so no one could hurt me. I'd never felt that before and I had not yet learned about God's promises of protection as the Bible says in:

Isaiah 41:10

Fear not, for I am with you; be not dismayed, for I am your God; I will strengthen you, I will help you, I will uphold you with my righteous right hand. ESV

Deuteronomy 31:6

Be strong and courageous. Do not fear or be in dread of them, for it is the Lord your God who goes with you. He will not leave you or forsake you. ESV

Even in situations where it feels and looks like we are alone, God is with us. However, if a performance-based, religious upbringing has skewed our perception of God, it's hard to believe that God wants anything to do with us when we blow it. My Christianity was definitely based on performance, and I wasn't doing so well.

Graham Cooke says:

"Christians with a performance mentality do everything to feel accepted and acceptable to God. We should serve Him out of gratitude, for there is nothing we can do to earn God's love."

I was running on a path that took me as far from God as I could possibly get. The path I had grown up on where God was shoved down my throat wasn't the path I wanted to walk on anymore. The very person God put on this earth to protect me, hurt me the most and taught me that God was a scary God. I didn't want to know or love a scary God or abide by His rules; I just wanted Him to stay away from me.

As I danced, and I watched married men from the community come into the club, I wondered if their wives knew they were there. You might think that only men who appeared to be losers or messed up at some level would go to a place to see women dance. That's not the case. I saw husbands, pastors, business owners, and otherwise upstanding men in the club at night. It's a crazy underground life for the men and the girls. People end up in those places because some other part of their life is broken and not working very well. I met a lot of girls who ended up dancing because they didn't know what else to do or once they started they didn't know how to get out. Once a girl starts dancing, the money comes in night after night, and it's easy to get used to that and get trapped in the lifestyle.

That part of my life is long over, but I still think of the girls and women trapped in the dark grip of dancing. It's important to me to reach out to the girls who are still in clubs in my town and elsewhere. Often, they don't get out until someone comes to help them. There are ministries like JC Girls and WINGS who help girls and women get out and restart their lives when they make the choice to quit.

Women who dance in those places are often harshly judged. However, we are not called to judge them; we are called to love them. Only God knows what type of hurt and devastation happened in their lives that landed them in the situation. Trauma, abuse, abandonment, and rejection are hard on the heart and soul and can send someone searching for healing and love in crazy places. Seeking for healing, they do more damage. It's not just damage to the body; it's damage to the mind, identity, and spirit.

> *"Our biggest hindrance has been that we have not understood the fullness of who we are in Christ or Who Christ is in us. Understanding this is the key to our transformation. We are in Christ, learning to be Christ- like and learning to abide in what He has already done for us. We are learning to face everything from the place of who we are in Jesus processing everything through His majesty. And Christ is in us, living through us, displaying the Father's glory for all to see."* –Graham Cooke

The woman with the issue of blood received two gifts the day she encountered Jesus, her healing and her identity. Before she was healed by Jesus, she was known as the outcast, the unclean woman. I'd bet that very few people knew her real name.

After she was healed, she may have been known as the woman who Jesus called *daughter* or the woman who *used* to bleed all the time or the woman who *used* to live outside the community. Do you see what I mean? When we are touched by Jesus, He changes our name and our identity. He changes how we are known.

It's the same with the girls who dance or girls who do other things because of the hurt or brokenness they have experienced in life. When they are touched by Jesus, he changes how they are known. They may have been called Buffy in the club, but once they encounter the true love of Christ, He gives them a new "real" name. Like the woman with the issue to blood, He saves them from something they could not get out of on their own. No one wakes up one morning and decides to dance for a living. It's a gradual process that comes from being made to feel like you're worthless that leads you to those kinds of decisions.

God knew that one day I would be talking to girls with crazy stories like mine, and I would completely understand them! God had a plan for me when I didn't have a plan for myself.

I never imagined that God would use my wounded life to help other women escape the pitfalls that their deep inner wounding would lead them into. In fact, I never thought God would want anything to do with me. I ran as far away from Him as I could, and He still had His hand of protection on me. He chose to have mercy and compassion on me.

He says in Jeremiah 29:11 "I know the plans that I have for you…" and Acts 10:34 says that "He is not a respecter of persons and shows no favoritism." His love extends to even the least of us. I felt that I was the chief among sinners, definitely the least of humanity.

The Bible talks about Rahab. She was an *active* prostitute. She was not all cleaned up and doing the right thing, yet she was responsible for helping the children of Israel defeat the enemy by protecting the spies sent out by Joshua.

From Joshua Chapter 2:

And Joshua the son of Nun sent[a] two men secretly from Shittim as spies, saying, "Go, view the land, especially Jericho." And they went and came into the house of a prostitute whose name was Rahab and lodged there. ² And it was told to the king of Jericho, "Behold, men of Israel have come here tonight to search out the land." ³ Then the king of Jericho sent to Rahab, saying, "Bring out the men who have come to you, who entered your house, for they have come to search out all the land." ⁴ But the woman had taken the two men and hidden them. ESV

Rahab had a prostitution ring going on in her house when the spies showed up. Of all the people God could have picked to help the men, *He picked the prostitute!*

I was a broken girl who stood on a stage every night and sold her body for men to look at. Now, I know that God loved me then just as much when I stood on that stage as He loves me now when I stand on the stage in a church to share about what He has done with the ashes of my life. It may be hard to believe, but it's true for you, too. When God sees you, He sees someone He loves. He loves you no matter your past or your present.

And he said, "I will make all my goodness pass before you and will proclaim before you my name 'The Lord.' And I will be gracious to whom I will be gracious and will show mercy on whom I will show mercy. Exodus 33:19 ESV

I danced for almost two years and all the while I felt hopeless and unworthy. And then one night when I was getting ready to go to work, I got a horrible pain in my stomach.

End Part One
Prayer

Thank you, God, for your saving grace and your love. Thank you for including the story of the woman with the issue of blood and how you made a way for her to come close to You to be healed. Help me to have the courage to do the same and to believe You love me and haven't forgotten about me. Help me to come close to You and to be healed. No matter how many people were around Jesus, healing came to the one who reached out to touch him.

Help me to have the faith she had and be determined to get my healing even if I must step out of my comfort zone to get there! Help me, Lord, to reach out for your touch to heal my hurt and brokenness and help me to know your true love for me. I'm learning that You do love me and don't require me to perform, only to receive.

In Jesus' name,
Amen

Scriptures:

God is our refuge and strength and abundantly available in time of need. Psalm 46:1 (Amp)

You, O Lord are a compassionate and gracious God, slow to anger abounding in love and faithfulness. Psalm 86:15

PART TWO

TESTING, TRIALS, AND TRIUMPH

I danced because it was a means to an end. I didn't think about what I was doing or about how I was keeping God at arms distance. I just wanted Him to leave me alone. I wasn't mad at Him or anything. I just didn't want much to do with Him.

I've since learned that God is not so good at leaving us alone—even when we want Him too!

I thought I didn't need Him, that is until the day when I started to have the most excruciating pain I'd ever felt. I was at home getting ready to go dance the same as I had done many days before when I got this terrible pain in my stomach. It made me double over in agony; the intensity crushed me. I didn't know what it was, and I didn't know what to do. Was I dying?

After not talking to God for almost two years that I'd been dancing, I now desperately needed Him to hear me. I cried out to Him for help. I wanted the pain to stop. I knew He was mad at me, and I thought I deserved every bit of pain I was feeling. The more I cried out to Him, the worse the pain got. This went on for almost forty-five minutes. I tried everything I knew to make the pain stop and it seemed like asking God to help me was not working either. I finally just asked God to kill me to make it stop, but the pain just intensified. This was my punishment. I should have known this would happen! I deserved this. Nothing was working. I then did the only thing left that I knew to do. In total desperation, I made a vow to God. I told Him if he would make the pain go away, I would never dance again.

To my surprise, He heard my cry. In less than sixty seconds, the pain stopped! One minute I was doubled over crying out, the next minute the pain was gone, and it never returned.

The pain that was ripping through my body a few minutes earlier stopped after I made the vow to God. I didn't know where the pain had come from, but I knew now that I wasn't dying, and that God heard me and helped me. He'd kept His promise. Now, I had to keep mine. What had I done? This would not be an easy thing to do. This life was all I had known for two years. I felt safe where I was and didn't want to lose that. Why did God help me? Wasn't He trying to punish me a few minutes beforehand? Maybe He didn't hate me after all. I knew what I had to do. After I got to my feet, I called the club where I was working and quit. They were shocked and tried to convince me to come back, but I had no intention of going back. I was serious about the promise I made to God. To make sure that I wouldn't give in to the temptation to go back, I took my duffle bag that held all my expensive costumes and makeup out of the back of the closet and threw it in the dumpster. That was really the end for me. I never danced again. I never entered a club again as a dancer, only as a rescuer of dancers.

I quit dancing, but it's not like the world suddenly came together in any order. I was lost. I needed to find a way to make my life into something that worked. That's when God started drawing me back to Him. I could feel that He wanted *ME*. He wanted me even though I was ashamed of myself. For the first time, I felt His Amazing Grace! I'd sang the words to Amazing Grace many times as a child, but I never understood them until then. I had to learn a new way of thinking about God, a new way to trust and, most importantly, a new way to love.

I went from making money as a dancer to working a lot of odd jobs. I briefly worked at Olive Garden as a waitress. I had to memorize the complete food and drink menu. The food menu was not a problem, but when it came to memorizing the alcohol portion, I just couldn't get it. I'd never had a drink and was not familiar with anything to do with drinking. After giving it the best try I could, I had to quit. It was hard making money, and what I did make was nowhere near what I made as a dancer. When I was dancing, I spent everything that came in each night because I figured that there was more where that came from. I didn't know dancing would be a short-lived part of my life. I had a little money saved, but not much. Certainly, not enough to start my life over again.

Eventually, I ran into a guy who had connections in the airline industry. He knew how I could apply to become a flight attendant. I got the job and worked for about a year with the airline. I'd always thought that it would be a glamorous job, but after doing it for a while, I felt that I was a glorified waitress. I was out of town all the time and not moving forward in my professional life.

There was a turning point when I left that job. I found work that I was very good at and that paid well. I went into sales. I started out selling dental plans and took first place as Sales Person of the Year three years in a row, defeating a woman who had previously held that title for many years before me. When I make up my mind to do something, I'm naturally driven and determined to succeed.

Someone told me that I would never be able to be a success in sales. That's all it took for me to prove them wrong. It came out that the woman who always held the title as the top performer before me was cheating, which meant her previous wins weren't wins at all! I was asked if I wanted to have her disqualified, my answer was "absolutely not." I was going to surpass any record she had ever set by working hard and honestly. The next month my sales doubled. At twenty-three years old, I was making a lot more money than most people my age made. My income still didn't surpass what I made as a dancer, but I was doing legitimate and respectable work.

Looking back, it is obvious that God was with me, not because I was doing anything good or doing anything bad. He was with me because He always loves us and is always with us. Not only was I a success in my work, but I had also gotten my dad's attention. Yes, with everything that had happened between us, I still wanted his love and approval. He was also in sales, and he was proud of me for doing well in that business. The first year that I won the sales competition, he sent me a big cookie bouquet with a card telling me how proud he was of me. I remember going to bed that night thinking that I'd had the most perfect day of my life. It felt good to know that dad was proud of me.

Once again, I connected performance with love.

This happens to people when they are taught that God's love is based on performance or how hard we work for it. The truth is, God does not need us to perform for Him. Many Christians are taught, directly or indirectly, that they must perform to receive God's love. That is an exhausting way to live.

Mark DeJesus, in his article *10 Toxic Stages of Performance-Based Christianity* (see Appendix D) explains what performance-based Christianity is and why it's so harmful. According to him, the stages are:

Stage 1: Feeling a lack of Love and Identity - Performance is a requirement for love.

Stage 2: Counterfeit Mindsets – You're not sure of who you are so you pretend or fabricate.

Stage 3: Performance-Based Living Becomes a Way of Life – You are always "on".

Stage 4: Performance Living Kick Back – Performance-based living wears a person out, it's exhausting.

Stage 5: Lack of Fulfillment – Performers feel lonely and unfulfilled when it comes to love.

Stage 6: Addiction Enters – In the absence of unconditional love and acceptance the performer looks for something to fill the void.

Stage 7: Shame and guilt are felt.

Stage 8: More performance
Stage 9: The Crash – The performer can't keep going on like this.
Stage 10: Cycle Restarts – Without help and a touch from Jesus, the performance starts all over again! *More details of these stages are in the back of this book. I highly recommend reading through them if you struggle with performance-based love.*

At one time or another, we may find ourselves performing for love. That's a normal experience; we get in trouble when we live in the performance cycle. Living as a full-time performer blocks us from receiving the gift of love that God has for us. Remember the woman with the issue of blood? She got to the point that she would do whatever it took to reach out to Jesus no matter how it looked or what people said. Jesus didn't rebuke her, He called her daughter, and He healed her. It's the same for us. He commended her for her faith, for stepping out and taking the risk to touch just the hem of His garment. God continues to heal me and love me completely. I'm still growing in the understanding of His love for me and letting go of the lingering traces of performing.

I continued to do well in my sales career which led to an invitation to join another company selling life insurance. I realized that I had a gift to sell, especially when I believed in what the product or service was. I went on to get my insurance license. I briefly worked for a small agency. I'd learned so much in ninety days that I left and started my own company, Texas Health Plans. I had no idea how to do what I did. I had no money; I had to get a Small Business Administration loan and pay a girl that came from the other office with me. I was living proof that when God says all things are possible with Him, it's true. He gave me supernatural strength to do what I did in the insurance business. I grew that business from 1996–2017. Looking back, I think I was in training for what He would have me do further down the road.

I was getting sensitive to the Lord and wanted to grow in my faith. I started going to Ed Young Jr.'s church that met in a theater. I remember going to his church and not feeling out of place.

There were lots of people coming to the Lord for the first time and others who were coming back to Him after being away from Him. At the time of this writing, if you go to Fellowshipchurch.com, the first thing you will see are the words:

You Belong Here. There were a lot of people who may have felt out of place at other churches, but at this church, we just felt like we belonged. I belonged.

God was wooing me by showing me His goodness. I was waiting for the lightning bolt to strike me as if the sins of my past had followed me. I was still learning to trust God and growing in my love for Him. I was not completely convinced that He was not angry at me. I almost felt hypocritical, but that didn't stop His love. He knew I was seeking Him. He brought people into my life to teach me lessons or to show me things that I didn't know. I wanted to know God better, and I wanted to meet a nice guy, get married and have a family. I poured out my heart to the Lord in one of my journals:

Dear Jesus,

> *Here I sit late on a Saturday evening listening to Christian music about a couple watching their children grow up. Less than a week ago I had a surgery that was to determine whether I would ever have an opportunity to have children of my own. I just broke up with my boyfriend; I was starting to depend on him instead of You, I'm sorry. I want so badly to have an awesome relationship with You. I just don't seem to know how to get there. I'm not sure of anything right now. I wish You would make some things very clear to me so that I may know a direction to turn and begin going forward, but I have no idea how. Please make Your will clear to me.*

> *God, please help nothing major to be wrong with me. I would love to be able to have a little baby, preferably a girl to love and cherish. I pray that You would make that possible. Please bring the father of my children to me quickly, if not, please give me peace while you prepare me for that stage in my life.*

> *Keep me close to You, Lord. Help nothing to come between us ever again. I have been close to You before, and there is no*

feeling like it. I miss You, Lord. I am sorry to have strayed away from You. Jesus, please help me get up in the morning and go to church. I would love to meet some good Christian friends and begin some meaningful friendships.

You are the missing ingredient, Lord. Please take me back and keep me close to You. Lord, thank you for all your blessings; help me to focus on them instead of worrying. I've tried to find my way on my own. I will never succeed without You. Every good thing in my life is because of You. Thank You for blessing my business week after week. You're so faithful. Help me to be faithful to You from now until forever.

I love you, Jesus,
Wendi

I would date guys from my singles group only to find that they were no different than the guys that I met in the clubs. I had changed my environment but was still getting the same results. Men saw me as an object, not a woman to be treasured. I wanted to meet a Christian man who was godly and took his faith seriously.

There was a singles pastor at our church. I admired him as a leader and thought that going out with him would be different than the other guys—*meaning*, I didn't expect that his hands would be all over me. I was wrong. We went on our date, and he did just what the other guys would do. He was no different.

Normally when something like this happened, I would feel helpless and turn into that eleven-year-old who had no power and no voice. With this man, I spoke up and told him that I was disappointed in him and thought that he would be different than the other guys. I told him that I didn't respect him as a leader and asked him to take me home. About an hour after he dropped me off, there was a knock on my door. He returned, and he was so broken. He apologized. He thanked me for confronting him and told me how God's conviction was upon him. I forgave him and from that point on we became like brother and sister. He won back my respect by taking responsibility for his actions. He was the first leader in my life to admit that he was wrong. No one ever came back to apologize or even take responsibility for what they had done to me. It turns out that he *was* different!

A few years later, after I'd started my insurance agency, he came to work for me. I had a young business without all the benefits that his previous place of employment had to offer. He would ask me about our "retirement" plan. I thought it was funny and would tell him that there was no retirement plan to speak of, but he kept asking.

GOD CHOOSES FOR ME

The retirement plan was an ongoing topic with my new hire, Steve. One day, while we were out of the office for a training meeting, he thought it would be a good idea to visit his financial planner. I had no time for this and couldn't figure out what part of "no retirement plan" he was not getting.

It was obvious to me that he was not going to drop the subject. He asked me again if we could stop by his financial guy's office to talk about a retirement plan. I gave in to his pressure and agreed to stop for a few minutes before my next meeting.

I wasn't expecting a man in a partial body cast to come around the corner. Jim had been in a rollerblading accident and looked like he was on the losing end of the battle. We sat down. He and Steve start talking about retirement stuff. I remember thinking how young Jim looked and guessed that he was probably no older than twenty-one. I had never met a twenty-one-year-old as smart as Jim. I even thought that he might be smarter than my dad, and I had never met anyone that I thought was smarter than my dad.

In the middle of his retirement plan talk I interrupted him and asked his age. "How old are you?" I was twenty-eight at the time, and he told me he was thirty. My disbelief was visible; I refused to take his word for it and asked to see his driver's license. He was indeed thirty with a very charming baby face. This was the guy who was going to solve our on-going retirement plan issue?

I checked the time, noticing that I needed to leave to get to my meeting. Steve and I rushed out of the office. When we got in the car, I told Steve that his friend was cute. I still don't know if he intended for us to meet that day for reasons other than the retirement plan.

By this time my heart was growing closer to God. I was learning more about Him and His love. There was a weekly Bible study that met at my house that Steve attended. We invited Jim to come, and I was delighted that he did! Jim was nice, and he seemed different.

After the Bible study, I knew I wanted to get to know him, so I invited him to go to a Michael English concert with a bunch of my friends. Surprised that he said yes, I had to scramble and try to find friends to go with us. Everyone was busy except one guy. Jim came to my house for what was supposed to be a group outing but only the three of us showed up. The concert was great. Jim will tell you that I spent most of the time in line waiting to get an autograph from Michael English (I was quite smitten with him!). After the concert my friend left, and Jim and I were at my house. I was ready for him to take off his "good guy" mask and start acting like everyone else. We were alone. He didn't try anything! He wasn't inappropriate, nothing strange or weird. He was the same nice guy he'd been from the moment I met him. I wondered what was wrong with him.

I liked him.

And for a change, I was the one who made the first move. I pulled him over to me and kissed him. It happened quickly, especially since we had only seen each other on three occasions, but unlike other guys, he didn't scare me. It felt natural to be with him. I didn't yet know if he was the one, but I knew he was different and that I felt safe. We started seeing each other almost every day. I quickly fell in love with him but was cautious; I didn't want my heart broken again.

I had a history of breaking up with other people, but I never thought of breaking up with Jim. I was falling more in love with him every day. I was also falling in love with Jesus. Love was healing my heart through Jesus and through this "normal" man in my life.

Again, I reflected on the words to the song Amazing Grace. If you have ever been through anything or done anything that left you feeling overwhelmed, broken, disappointed or simply out of control read these words and see if you can sense, as I did, the peace of God washing over you, releasing hope where there was no hope or perhaps forgiveness where you felt none before.

> Amazing grace! how sweet the sound
> That saved a wretch like me!
> I once was lost, but now am found,
> Was blind, but now I see.
>
> T'was grace that taught my heart to fear,
> And grace my fears relieved;
> How precious did that grace appear
> The hour I first believed!
>
> Through many dangers, toils, and snares,
> I have already come;
> T'was grace that's brought me safe thus far,
> And grace will lead me home.
>
> The Lord has promised good to me,
> His word my hope secures;
> He will my shield and portion be
> As long as life endures.
>
> Yes, when this flesh and heart shall fail,
> And mortal life shall cease;
> I shall possess, within the veil,
> A life of joy and peace.

The earth shall soon dissolve like snow,
The sun forbear to shine;
But God, who called me here below,
Will be forever mine.
John Newton, Olney Hymns, 1779

I had deep feelings of guilt and shame, but I was starting to feel His love and grace even though I didn't do anything to deserve it or earn it. God gives us grace because He loves us.

Ephesians 2:8-9

[8] *For by grace you have been saved through faith. And this is not your own doing; it is the gift of God,* [9] *not a result of works, so that no one may boast. ESV*

In each kindness from God, I learned more about His grace, but I wasn't fully ready to embrace His love because I didn't know how.

Phillip Holmes from Desiring God expounds on grace:

God's Grace Is Not Like Man's Grace
Part of how we view God's grace is often birthed out of our experiences with each other. Whether it's a parent, relative, or our general view of mankind, our experience with sinful and broken people affect our view of our holy and righteous God. We're unacquainted with grace, mercy, and truth that's untainted by sin. Humanly speaking, though we've experienced grace, we've never met a person that embodied grace perfectly.

As I reflected on how we love and show grace, two things stood out to me about man and our motivation to forgive:

- *Natural man is motivated to be gracious because man is aware (to some extent) that he's as guilty as the person in need of grace.*
- *Natural man forgives others because he often only knows a small piece of all the other person is actually guilty of.*

46

I'm sure there are more human motivations for showing grace, but from these alone we discover two factors that play enormous parts in our ability to forgive—our own sin and ignorance.

As I began to process this, I was blown away. God is a holy and righteous God, completely void of sin, full of goodness and love. He has never made a mistake and can do anything but fail. He is perfect in all ways. Every time I think of this reality, I'm brought to tears. Like Phillip Holmes, I too am often baffled by God's grace and His ability to see the good in me when I can't see it myself.

LEARNING TO TRUST

After the concert, we started dating. It wasn't long after that, we were engaged and then married. Letting a man close to me again was not easy. I had major trust issues. Jim's relationship with God was very solid. He can hear from the Lord, and he trusts what he hears. He doesn't have to go through the sorting process of trying to figure things out like I do. He's very strong in his faith, and he does not waver. He's a private man and would never boast about anything. He was committed to loving the Lord and supporting me.

I was still wounded by the rejection of my dad choosing someone else over me. Even though I cared for Jim, I didn't know what it was like to be chosen by a good man. I had dated a few guys before him and was engaged twice, but nothing came of those relationships. I wanted the man who married me to be my knight in shining armor and rescue me from the nightmare I had lived since I was eleven years old. Now there was a man in my life, and I wondered if he would love me or hurt me like the rest.

Jim was oddly different—*he was normal.* When I told people about him, the word I used over and over to describe him was "normal." For the first two or three months that we were together, I would tell people that he must be on the FBI's most wanted poster, and I just hadn't found it yet. He was too good to be true.

He wasn't prideful, didn't flirt with other girls, called when he said he would, and did what he said he would do. It was weird to me because I wasn't used to being treated with such respect.

Maybe Jim was normal, but I had baggage from my past that was anything but normal. I had not been hurt by strangers who happened upon me at some point in life. I had been hurt by people close to me, people I should have been able to trust to take good care of me. Trust? What was trust? How do I go from no first-hand knowledge of what it meant to trust someone, to feel safe enough to allow a man to be close to me? I knew how to go through the motions, but in the back of my mind, I still had the "rules" that I learned in church. Those rules followed me around like a taunting bully. Which one would I break that would get me eternal punishment? Would it be the clothes I wore, the music I listened to or the magazine I read? If I did a normal thing like drink a glass of wine, I believed I would go straight to Hell. I was surprised to find that a sip of wine didn't cause me to spontaneously combust.

I didn't know it at the time, but God placed Jim in my life to help me heal. He used him to challenge my belief system and my mindset. I had dysfunctional ways of thinking that I thought were normal. Until Jim, no one had pointed them out or called me on them. I had a lot of illusions about my dad and still had him on a pedestal like he was when I was a little girl. God used Jim to help me see my dad and the damage that he caused in my life more clearly. I had every reason to hate my dad and to think the absolute worst things about him, but I didn't. I had created someone who I loved to *imagine* my dad was. The person he was in my pretend memory wasn't the same in reality. If I were ever going to get past what happened, I'd have to first admit the truth. The Scriptures tell us that freedom comes by knowing the truth.

John 8:32

And you will know the truth, and the truth will set you free. ESV

I repeatedly made excuses for my dad. I wasn't willing to face the truth. My dad treated me differently than the other kids, and it was hurtful. I thought if I just kept doing things his way he would eventually see me and love me. Jim saw that I was not operating in truth, and because of it, I was not able to experience the freedom I deeply longed for.

For several years at the beginning of our marriage, it was the only thing that we ever fought about. No matter what my dad did, I would defend him to the death. These weren't just little disagreements; they were all out heated conflicts.

The moment Jim met my dad, he saw him for who he was, not as the infallible man I pretended he was. We had many conversations about how my dad treated me. What was obvious to Jim was not clear to me. Were we talking about the same person? Even though my dad would hurt my feelings and make me cry, I never confronted him or told him how he was hurting me, which did not sit well with my husband.

There was one time when my parents flew my sister in from New York to visit them. They knew in advance that she was coming, but it wasn't until they picked her up from the airport and were on their way to the restaurant that they called Jim and I to invite us to join them. I didn't think much of it until I went out to the backyard where Jim was working to tell him that we needed to go have lunch with my sister, dad and step-mom. Jim was shocked at the last-minute invitation. He was not going to jump through the hoop that I'd always jumped through when it came to my dad.

He said, "You mean he just now called us and wants us to be there in thirty minutes? Call them back and tell them we are not going." His words were like a ringing gong in my ears. Did he just say what I thought he said? He told me to call my dad, say "no" to him and tell him why? I was furious. Jim was serious about not going no matter what I said. He helped me see the disregard that my dad had for us by showing me that they had every opportunity to call us in advance if they really wanted us at that lunch. Jim was not going along with the dysfunctional behavior, even over something little, that I willingly accepted in my relationship with my dad.

For the first time in my life, I called my dad, and I stood up to him. I told him that Jim was not going to allow us to be a part of his last-minute afterthought invitation to lunch and that we would not be there. I was angry, and he knew it. He was silent on the other end of the line. He had never heard me speak to him like that in my entire life. For thirty years, he had controlled me; for thirty years, it was always what he wanted. He was used to me taking whatever kind of treatment that he gave me. Even though I'd gone along with it in the past, that day I finally said "no" to the way he treated me, even though it was Jim's decision. He was forcing me to stand up to my dad, and I wasn't happy about any of it.

That kind of behavior had become commonplace for my dad. Sometimes he would invite me to lunch, and of course, I always went. I never turned down a chance to spend time with him. Those times were important to me but didn't seem too important to him. He was very busy. When he finally took time out of his busy schedule to see me, he spent much of the lunch hour on his phone. I wanted some connection with him, so I would take whatever he gave me, even if he did talk on the phone during our lunch. At least he was there. I thought I deserved to be neglected and treated poorly. He was my daddy. However, a daddy should make their daughter feel treasured and like a princess. I never felt any of that from my dad.

Many girls who have been abused feel the same way. The abuse teaches them to think less of themselves, to allow others to mistreat them and to never speak up about it. They often cry in silence feeling trapped and lonely inside. They don't know their worth or their value. Sometimes it takes a person like Jim or a friend, mentor or family member to show them the truth in a way that they can understand. They have scars that no one can see and many times they are still experiencing the pain from the abuse.

I had scars that no one could see. Inner scars can take a long time to heal. It can be easy to stuff hurts down so far that it feels like they are healed, but the truth comes out when something reminds us of or touches that hurt place. I didn't want my past to interfere with my marriage, but I didn't know how to keep it from happening. I'm so thankful for Jim. He is a kind and patient man with his heart set on my healing and freedom. He didn't just talk about God's love; he showed me God's love. Jim came to know the Lord when he was in college. His relationship with God was and always has been very solid and very private. He has a firm trust in Him. When he hears from God, he doesn't waver. He obeys and moves forward. Where I go back and forth with a thousand questions, Jim stands firm. I'm sure this is a large part of why I trusted him enough to let him closer than I'd ever let anyone else before.

I was glad to have Jim but being close to him required me to peel back layers of my heart, and it hurt. Layer after layer of feelings that I'd refused to acknowledge about my dad came to the surface. I couldn't hide them because I was married to someone who wanted to get to the truth and not play my pretend games. I was angry at my dad, and I was angry at my husband for refusing to live in my pretend world. I had built a thick wall of protection around my heart that still stung from the emotional and spiritual abuse suffered at the hands of my dad. Even though I love Jim with all my heart, and I know God sent him to me, I still struggled to be physically close to him without shutting down. What God intended to be the most beautiful act of love that two people could share was damaged in me. I had to learn the difference between an act of hurt and an act of love.

OUR FAMILY

B oth Jim and I were ready to start our family. It wasn't long before our first son Jace was born, and two years later our son Jaxon was born.

I wanted to be a mom, but I didn't want my children to have a childhood like mine. It was important that they knew they were loved and that we were always there for them. I didn't want them to question our love no matter what they did or didn't do.

For the first eight months of Jace's life, I stayed home with him. He was doing so well that I talked to Jim about going back to work part-time. We both agreed that things were going smoothly at home and my going back to work wouldn't take away from his care. We decided that I would go back to work, but I'd work from home. This allowed me to simply walk down the hall to see my baby. I also had a little help with him a few times a week, so I could get more work done and help Jim with the finances.

My business did very well, but I missed being with my son. I was torn between wanting to work and wanting to be with him. I prayed and asked God what He thought would be best for our son. I didn't want Jace to be pushed aside in any way as we both led our busy lives building our businesses. This was such a concern to me that when Jace was thirteen months old, I wrote this letter to him in my journal:

Hi, Pumpkin! I just wanted to write you to let you know some of the things that have been on my mind lately. You are a little over thirteen months old, and I am really struggling with the decision to continue working. For the first eight months of your life, it was just you and I all day long! You slept a lot during that time, so I thought it might be good if I went back to work part-time. I discussed it with your daddy, and he thought that would be fine. The Lord has really been good to us and has blessed my business unbelievably in the last five months. The problem I'm facing though is now I am working a lot more than I thought I would or intended to, and I wonder if the time away from you is what Jesus wants for you and me. I struggle with the possibility of selling my insurance business and just using that money to buy a house that we don't have to make payments on, so I can spend all my time with you. It seems like God has blessed both of my businesses so much. He is continuing to send me business for a reason. Maybe I'm supposed to keep working? I feel badly for every minute that I don't spend with you. I am not sure which way the Lord is leading me, so I am still praying about it! Please know, Sweetheart, whatever decision I make will be a tough one and will determine a lot about your life. It will determine the neighborhood we live in, the school you go to, and the amount of time you and I will be able to spend together. I love you more than anything in this world, more than any possession I could ever dream of and I want to make the right choice for us. You are the most precious gift I could ever have been blessed with. I love you with all my heart.

Love,
Your Mommy

It may seem that writing a letter to a thirteen-month-old was a little crazy, but I knew one day my son would read it and know what I was thinking and feeling about him from the moment he was born. Children should never have to guess how their parents feel about them or wonder if the love they receive is based on circumstances or performance. When a child is raised that way, it sets them up for a possible life of uncertainty or insecurity.

This was only one of many journal entries I wrote to or about my children. In my journals, I captured my thoughts, feelings and sometimes my prayers. I look back now, and I'm glad that I have several journals filled with "mom" entries! I have such deep love for my children.

Being a parent has helped me realize how God feels about us. In His Word, He is always telling us how He feels about us! He wants the very best for His children and always works things together for our good even when we don't know it.

Romans 8:28

And we know that for those who love God all things work together for good,[a] for those who are called according to his purpose. ESV

That's the heart of the Heavenly Father.

I believe God allows us to become parents so we get a real-life example of how much we love our children. Our love is not a perfect love like His so it's even more amazing that He loves me perfectly.

I learned more of God's loving care and kind heart for me as I loved my boys. I was starting to see God in a different way. He was becoming a God of my present instead of a God of the past. He would never cast me aside, hurt me or use me. He saw me the very same way that He saw the woman with the issue of blood, as His beloved daughter. For years, I chased the love of my earthly father only to come up short, never finding the love I thought I desperately needed. God's love is different; He *wants* to be found when we seek Him. I am so thankful that I never received the unconditional love and approval of my earthly father. If I had, I would've settled for that. Instead, that yearning for unconditional love and approval led me on a journey to find the Heart of my Heavenly Father. His love and approval come with no strings attached, and it's a pure, innocent and safe love!

Proverbs 8:17 says:

I love those who love me,
and those who seek me diligently find me. ESV

Deuteronomy 4:29-31 says:

But from there you will seek the Lord your God and you will find Him, if you search after Him with all your heart and with all your soul. ³⁰ When you are in tribulation, and all these things come upon you in the latter days, you will return to the Lord your God and obey His voice. ³¹ For the Lord your God is a merciful God. He will not leave you or destroy you or forget the covenant with your fathers that He swore to them. ESV

Jeremiah 29:13

"You will seek Me and find Me when you search for Me with all of your heart". ESV

I have a picture taped to my mirror. It's an image of Jesus embracing a young girl; her head is resting on His shoulder as He closely embraces her. They both have their eyes closed. The little girl looks like she is relieved that she is finally safe in the loving arms of Jesus. In the picture, Jesus is strong and safe. He's holding her like a daddy would hold his little girl. On the back of the picture, I wrote these words:

"This is what I long to feel from my Heavenly Father!"

Not far away, on another wall, I have a plaque that says:

"You are loved for the little girl you were, for the special woman you are and the precious daughter you will always be." To this day, these are reminders of God's heart toward me.

WILLING TO BE WILLING

Even with my precious sons Jace and Jaxon, my family somehow didn't seem complete. Deep inside I longed for a daughter. My heart was starting to hurt from the longing that I couldn't push away. I watched my friends have baby girls, and I was sincerely happy for them, but with each new celebrated baby girl that a friend or family member had, I was reminded of my prayer for us to have a daughter of our own.

I was trusting God to make it all right, which meant I wanted Him to make me all right with or without a daughter.

Jim's mom had never met the kids. He wanted her to meet them and at least have a chance to get to know them. But I didn't want them to meet her because once they did they would wonder where she'd been and why she wasn't in their lives. At the time, they were very close to their other grandparents, Jim's dad and step-mom. I didn't want the boys to feel rejected by Jim's mom.

For months, I resisted Jim's request to go visit her. I told him that if she wanted to see them so bad, she could get on a plane and come see us. After all, she didn't even have to work, and we were both working full-time jobs and raising children. We didn't have any margin in our schedules. Jim said that would never have happened because of her drinking. She wouldn't be able to drink at our house like she could at hers. Even though I thought it was a bad idea, I finally agreed to go visit and did all the changing and rearranging of our schedules to make it happen.

When we landed at the airport, they were late picking us up. When they finally arrived, we all loaded into her smoke infested car, which was parked in a handicap parking space, where it was hard to even breathe. She was telling the kids that it was okay to park in the handicap parking, even though they were not supposed to. I didn't like that at all, so I tried to make a joke out of it by telling my kids that "grandma" was just kidding. That word was not one I used to describe her to my children. A real grandma would have been a part of their whole lives. We got to her house which was just as bad as the car. Jaxon couldn't even be in the house because of his smoke allergies. We had to go out and stand on the back porch. I was furious! I was sending my husband those "I'm not happy signals," and he knew exactly what they meant. I couldn't wait to get out of there.

By the time we got back to the hotel, I let him know that I was very upset and that this is exactly why I didn't want us to come. This environment was not right for the kids. I think deep down, Jim knew it too but was hoping that it would turn out okay. It wasn't okay; we were both frustrated. I continued to plead my case and expressed my strong desire to return home. Jim finally agreed that we could go home in the morning. It was all set, but before falling asleep, I said a prayer and told God that I didn't understand why we were there. I didn't like it one bit. I didn't want my kids there, but if He wanted us to stay that He had to make it clear because I was done and ready to go! There! I can at least say that I prayed about it and went to bed thinking we were going to get up, pack, and go home.

When I got up, I didn't know what happened to me! It was beyond strange. Just eight hours before, all I wanted to do was get us out of there. But I woke up with a complete change of heart and a bizarre compassion for her. Instead of rushing the kids to get packed so we could leave, I was rushing them so that we could go back to "grandma's" house, something that I'd refused to call her before! My attitude changed, and we had a great visit with

Jim's mom. That little prayer, though prayed hesitantly, showed God that I was at least *willing* to let Him change things and work in this situation. It taught me to trust how He speaks to me and taught me how to hear His voice even in difficult situations. That day, He wanted me to just be obedient and allow Him to change me. And, I was. Had I not been at least *willing*, I would have missed the whole blessing. This experience stays with me to this day because I learned how God will change my heart in a moment if I'm truly open to Him to do so.

THE STALKING STARTED ON
THE WAY TO WALMART

S hortly after we returned from the trip to visit Jim's mom, I was driving to Walmart. Thoughts of having a baby girl kept coming to my mind. I didn't know where they were coming from. I was getting frustrated with myself and questioned the motives of my heart. Was I enviously thinking of my friends who had baby girls? I didn't think so. I was always happy for my friends even though I hoped God would bless us with a daughter too.

As I was getting closer to Walmart, I heard something in my head that told me to prepare for and anticipate a baby girl and to take steps of faith about having a daughter. I didn't know what that meant. Was this my crazy brain again? Or was this the Lord speaking? I couldn't get rid of the thoughts. As I was driving and hearing those words in my heart, questioning if this was truly from the Lord, a van cut right in front of me. On the right side of the back window, there was a little sticker that said, "Step of Faith Dance Studio." Those were the exact words that God had given me! That's when I knew that I knew it wasn't my imagination. It was God asking me to take steps of faith and to be obedient by preparing for and anticipating our daughter. Jim and I were doing our part to have another child, and I didn't know what other acts of faith God meant.

He asked me what I would be doing to prepare for a baby girl if I knew I was pregnant right at that moment. I said that I would be buying things that were pink, I'd be painting a room for the baby and telling all my friends. He said then that's what I want you to do. "I want you to take steps of faith. Prepare for and anticipate her." I tried to explain to the Lord that here in the 21st century we did not announce our pregnancy to the world until at least the fourth month, especially at my age. It seemed wise to keep that information to ourselves in case there was a miscarriage or something went wrong. He very sweetly said to me, "Wendi, do you trust Me?" I answered Him, "Yes, I do trust You." Then He said to me, "Then get to it!"

When I got to Walmart, my first stop was in the baby department. Taking my first step of faith, I looked for something to buy for a baby girl that I believed the Lord told me was coming. Hoping to avoid anyone I knew, I picked out a little pink outfit that said "love." I hung the dress on Jim's vanity mirror and waited for him to come home. When I shared with him what happened, he nodded his head in agreement keeping any other thoughts he may have had to himself. I knew he wondered if I had lost my mind.

The next confirmation came about a week later. Once again, I was driving to Walmart. I was at the same intersection where I was when I saw the sticker the week before. Another car pulled in front of me at the same place and on the back of that car, there was a sticker that just said the word "Girl." The "I" was in the shape of a little girl and it was pink. A few days later, I saw the exact same sticker that said "Girl" Wow! I followed the car in front of me to a parking lot. When the woman got out of the car and went in to do her shopping, I got out of my car and took a picture of the sticker. God was showing me another sign. It was like He was stalking me (I say that with complete reverence). Or, as others have heard me say, "He was blonde-proofing it for me." The signs just kept coming.

Another confirmation came when we went on a trip to visit my brother in Georgia. While there, I was driving my kids around the neighborhood where I grew up. At one point, I had to turn around to head in a different direction, so I pulled into a driveway to make the turn. On the back of the car that was in the driveway was a sticker with just the word "Girl." There were no other words or descriptions on the sticker, it just said "Girl." I thought it was interesting that God not only showed me a "girl" sticker in Texas, but He also showed it to me in Georgia, which was another sign! It was evident to me that He was showing me girls and that our next baby was going to be a girl.

The signs continued to come. We were still in Georgia driving on the highway, and I was starting to get excited about seeing these signs all over the place. I was trying to understand what was going on, and at the same time, I was overwhelmed that God was doing this for me so that I would never doubt what He said even when things got difficult on the way to her arrival. The next sign came while we were on another drive. There was a car in front of us that had "girl" in the license plate. I took another picture. Confirmation!

The next sign was a little more personal. It came as a word of knowledge[1] from the associate pastor at my brother's church. The senior pastor taught his message. At the end of the service, the associate pastor addressed the whole congregation and said that he had gotten a word of knowledge for someone in the church. He went on to say that the person was fearful and concerned about having a miscarriage. I had never seen this man before in my life. He didn't know that I was concerned about being able to carry a baby full-term because of the surgery that I had when I was younger and because of my age. At the time, I was thirty-nine.

---

[1] Meaning: Among Pentecostal and Charismatic Christians, the word of knowledge is often defined as the ability of one person to know what God is currently doing or intends to do in the life of another person. It can also be described as knowing the secrets of another person's heart. Wikipedia

He said God told him to tell that person that they were not to live in fear but to focus on the promise. When I first heard that, I thought it was confirmation that I was not going to have a miscarriage but that's not what he said. His words were that I was not supposed to live in the "fear" of having one. It took me a while to understand his words, but later it would make more sense. I had never had a miscarriage before, but the fear of it was going through my mind. He said that he had more to share with that person and asked if they would come up to the front when the service closed. I knew he was talking about me. I bolted out of my seat up to the front to talk to him the second the closing prayer was over. God was committed to confirming His promise to me about having a little girl, and He didn't stop until I had no doubt left. Talking to the associate pastor after the service was even more confirmation on that trip.

When I got back from Georgia, I remembered that my friend was leading a Bible study. I had no idea when they were meeting, so I gave her a call to find out the details. As it turned out, the Bible study was that day. I was exhausted from my trip, but I decided to go anyway. I was about to have my final confirmation.

We were preparing for our little girl as God told us to do. We had even picked out her name: Jenna Leigh. We didn't know when she was coming, but we knew her name!

I walked into the house of the woman hosting the Bible study, and she said, "Hi, I'm Jenna." I could hardly believe what I was hearing. I asked what her middle name was, and of course—she was Jenna Leigh! I asked her how she spelled her middle name, and she said "L-e-i-g-h". Just like my Jenna's middle name, which was also my middle name. I just about fainted. I started to cry, and the friend I came with started to cry! We had a mini-Bible study right there in the entryway as I told them about all that God was doing in my life.

DID GOD SAY?

There was nothing in me that doubted what God spoke to me. How could I doubt when He confirmed His word to me so many times? I did what He said, I told people, took steps of faith, prepared and waited for the "any minute I'm pregnant" moment. One month passed, and nothing happened, but on Mother's Day, just a few weeks later, I took a pregnancy test and found out that I was pregnant!

I told my friends at church that I was going to have a girl; God was answering my prayers. To say I was happy does not come close to expressing the joy that I felt! I was so excited to know I was going to be a mommy again and this time to a little girl. God was fulfilling His promise to me. It wasn't long, however, until my excitement turned to heartbreak. We noticed that there were signs that the pregnancy was not progressing properly. My HCG levels were supposed to be doubling, but they weren't. Within a few weeks, I'd lost the baby. I was devastated. I'd never had a miscarriage, and I didn't know how to handle it. The doctor wanted to do a DNC, a procedure to "clean out" the womb where the baby stopped growing. I refused because I believed that God could do a miracle and bring my baby to life if that's what He wanted to do. I went back to my doctor a week later, and she told me that the process was complete, that my body had "cleaned" itself. I was still dealing with the emotional devastation of the loss, but I was physically healthy. She told me that my body was ovulating and there was no medical reason we could not try again.

There was no question that we were ready. Eighteen or twenty days later, we were pregnant again! It was Jim's birthday. I felt that it was God's way of telling me that He was proud of me for having faith in His promise. Once again, I went to church and told everyone. We were so excited! My brother and I were jumping up and down rejoicing at God's goodness to give us another baby.

My joy turned to sadness when a few weeks later I relived the loss all over again with the miscarriage of that baby. I could barely get out of bed. I'd lost all motivation for life. I didn't want to do anything. I'd never felt that low before. Fortunately, we had planned a family trip to Hawaii. It was there that the Lord began to heal the pain that allowed me to begin moving forward. In those days, I asked the Lord if He would close my womb if it were not time for me to have the baby that He promised. I still didn't doubt His Word to me; I just wanted it when it was His time not mine. I didn't want to keep getting pregnant and losing babies.

HE PROMISED

I struggled to make sense of what happened with the loss of two babies. I knew I had heard from God, and I believed Him to do what He promised. I just didn't understand what was going on. I poured my heart out in my journal when Jim was away on a business trip:

> It's been a hard three months for me with having the miscarriages. I've never gone through anything so painful in all my life, and I've been through some serious stuff. I don't like it when Jim is not here. Things just seem to be better with him at home. Who knows, maybe this time apart will be good for us, they say absence makes the heart grow fonder.
>
> It seems that all life revolves around my menstrual cycle and getting the timing of things just right. When I'm out, I see pregnant women, and I'm reminded of the two babies I just lost. Sometimes it's hard; either way, I still believe God's promise and the confirmations of our baby girl, who I've already named Jenna. The journey to Jenna continues, and I'm so excited to see how it's all revealed. I love You, Lord.

God was present in my life in every way. He was growing me and drawing me into a deeper relationship with Him. As I waited for Jenna, God was still moving me forward in wholeness and calling me to not only be a mom but to step into ministry by sharing the story of what happened to me with others, so they could be encouraged and receive healing. I'd never thought about my story helping others or about bringing a message of healing.

I'd been doing things to get ready for my daughter as God had instructed, but it wasn't happening. At the time, we had never considered adoption as an option. I knew what it was like to be in a family where some kids were step-kids and others were biological. As a step-child, I certainly wasn't treated the same by my step-mom. I'd already had two boys; I didn't want any child of mine to feel that they were any less lovable than another. I never wanted to make a child feel that way. I immediately disqualified myself as a potential adoptive mom.

I put it all back in God's hands and turned my attention to what I believed the Lord was asking me to do. He'd put on my heart to have a Healing & Restoration Service at my childhood church. The service was to be held at the church my dad used to pastor. I had previously tried to begin planning something, but I'd canceled it twice thinking that I'd be pregnant at the time of the service and wouldn't be able to do it. Looking closer, I was avoiding the event and trying to make my own plan instead of going with the plan God had put in my heart. I wanted to help some of the people in our old church move on and get closure from the past. It seemed that every time I would visit some of the people from my dad's church, they would ask a lot of questions about him. Some were asking to get gossip and really had no care or concern for my dad, while others were asking out of a genuine love for both my dad and our family. I knew my dad would never want to return to help them, so as his firstborn child, I was hoping that I could be a sufficient "stand-in." I was nervous, however, because many of the people really hated my dad. I wasn't trying to stir the pot, I only wanted to help them heal as God had helped me to heal.

A friend who didn't know what I was going through said she wanted to share something with me and gave me a word of knowledge. She told me that God was asking me to do something, and I was not being obedient. She went on to say that God had given me a promise and that He was not going to fulfill that promise if I didn't do what He asked me to do. I knew what she was talking about: The Healing & Restoration Service.

He was also asking me to do something else: to let go of my dad. I knew that my dad still didn't treat me well and that I had to confront him about it and take a break from having him in my life. The time had come for me to release him from any fantasy that I had about him being a nurturing, loving father to me. I had to let go so that I could move on and God could manifest His perfect plans and purposes for my life. I gave myself time to think and pray. I wasn't sure how I was going to do it. I believe God was getting my heart ready, but I was not quite there. In fact, two years prior, I had concluded that letting him go was the only way for me to move forward in a healthy, positive way. When preparing to do that, I wrote the following journal entry at that time with full intentions of saying good-bye to my dad.

From my journal:

I just wanted to put in writing the thoughts I am having just in case something was to happen to me before this situation gets resolved. It seems no matter how hard I try to resolve things with my dad, I always get hurt in the end. The rejection I feel from him is so overwhelming that it has affected my life for over 23 years, my marriage for 8 years and my relationship with my kids for almost 7 years.

I say, after 4 years of living in a different city than my dad, and almost 2½ years after I "let him go" at a balloon ceremony at The Road, that enough is enough. I believe, with all my heart, that it will never be the way I need it to be in his lifetime. I will forever be the "black sheep" of his family because he is unwilling to admit any kind of wrongdoing with regards to me and how he handled the divorce and bringing a new wife into the family with absolutely no regard to my feelings.

How can a man pick a woman he has only known, by his own recollection, for 2 to 3 years, over his own FIRSTBORN daughter who loved, adored and worshipped him? Even after sexually molesting her for 3 years while also pastoring the church she attended. I mean, seriously, what kind of a reaction was I supposed to have when a woman, claiming to be my friend, suddenly decides she is going to be my stepmother? All the while, her husband and my mom ran off together, and they were all sleeping together before anyone knew what was going on. In fact, I have a brother or sister somewhere in Heaven due to the miscarriage his now-wife had 4 months before we were told we were moving to Texas to "start a church." Can this story be true? Yes, this is the hell I have lived in my lifetime.

Along the way, I got another brother and sister that I was strategically kept away from. I had to call my dad for permission before I was allowed to stop by my own father's house. That made me feel very rejected. All my siblings LIVED in his home, but I could not even visit without permission. The only time I could even see my dad was if I went by his office or if his wife went out of town and he took me to dinner or a movie or something. That felt weird or like I was doing something wrong because, if she would call when we were together, he would tell me to be quiet so she couldn't hear me, and he never told her where he was or who he was with. I don't know what is wrong with my dad, but I have loved him unconditionally from the day I was born. I always will.

Now, I have my own family, and my husband and kids did not ask for any of this, yet they have stuck by me through the whole thing. I choose, now, to let go completely of my dad, so that I can focus on my family. It makes me sad that this is where this road led me, but I can truly say I have done my best to make things good with my dad, but I can't sacrifice my husband and kids any longer for that cause!

I pray that my siblings still want to have a relationship with me, but the loyalty this family has for dad is very strong! I know, because I led the pack in the "brutal loyalty" (as my brother put it at our rehearsal dinner) department. I pray that when the time comes for me to tell my 2 boys that they will still love their Papa and understand some of why mommy acts the way she does sometimes. I wish I could end with "And they lived happily ever after," but this is my story to date. By the grace and mercy of God, and with some distance and time away from dad, I believe my family will "live happily ever after," and that is what has brought me to this decision.

Right after writing this journal entry, the phone rang. It was my dad; he invited me to his 60th birthday party. So, I put off letting him go. I felt the Lord stopped me from making it happen because the time wasn't right. That phone call gave me a little hope that maybe things would get better between us. That hope lasted for about six months. And, it looked like it was indeed getting better, but in time, things faded back to the same old thing, and I felt like another rejection had happened.

A couple more years went by with more hurt and disappointment. With each one, I became more damaged because I thought it was my dad's love and approval that determined my value. God had a much better plan, and He was preparing me to receive something far greater than love and approval of any man or woman on this earth.

THE TURNING POINT

I continued planning the Healing & Restoration Service. I felt God was going to use me to minister to that church so they could have closure from my dad leaving many years ago. For the sake of the church, I had previously asked my dad to go back with me so people could get closure and move on. I knew that God would forgive my father and that his story might help men who struggled with the same issue. He refused to share his story and certainly didn't want me to share mine. I had a decision to make. I wasn't going to be able to do what my earthly father wanted me to do and still be obedient to my Heavenly Father. The decision was easy; I would obey my Heavenly Father.

The time had come. Jim and I went to have a conversation with my dad. I told him I was letting go of him and the expectation that I had of him being a father in my life. I would have expected to have had tears and feel deep sadness. That didn't happen. The second I let go, I felt like a filter was removed from my heart and God was flooding my spirit with an even deeper realization of His love for me. My eyes were open, and I knew that I no longer needed my dad's approval, something I'd longed for all my life. That's when I felt my spiritual life grow to a new level. I knew I didn't need any man to tell me what I was hearing from God. That day, the Holy Spirit became my Teacher.

Before leaving for the meeting with my dad, I wrote the following in my journal:

Well, I'm finally going to step out in faith and obey God in a couple of areas of my life. I believe he is asking me to do something that is long overdue but will be one of the hardest things I have ever done up to this point in my life. He's asking me to let go of my dad. I'm not sure how long it will be or if it will be forever. I don't believe that I can move forward in the blessing God has for me and still hold on to him. Today is the day I will say goodbye to him, Jim is going with me. We are meeting him halfway at lunchtime, and I pray that God will make me very strong and courageous and will not allow me to have second thoughts which are usually from the enemy.

I've been prophesied to that when I am obedient, God will bless us with two baby girls, Jenna and Jessa. God, You are amazing!

Once again, God's relentless love was at work on my behalf.

THE NIGHT OF THE HEALING & RESTORATION SERVICE

As I prepared my heart right before the Healing and Restoration Service, I wanted to reach out to my dad. I knew he was not going to read this at the moment I wrote it, but I thought he might read it one day and I wanted him to know how I felt and what was going on inside of me.

So, I wrote:

Dear Dad,

Well, I am sitting in Brandon's living room. We have just arrived here in Atlanta for the Healing & Restoration Service I told you about back in April last year. It is now the time for my final step of healing. I am coming out of the prison that I have allowed you to keep me in for the last 29 years! It has truly been a living hell at times, yet I would not change any of it. The journey, though quite painful, has brought me to the point in my life where my relationship with my Heavenly Father is stronger than it ever would've been without this experience. The ironic thing is, just like that relationship, I believe my relationship with you could also be stronger than it ever could've been without the events that occurred between us if you would allow God to do the work in you that He so desires!

Dad, you are a very gifted man with more potential than most people ever hope to have, but your pride and unwillingness to do the right thing by those you have hurt very deeply are keeping you from the true blessings God has waiting for you!

I am still believing the vision that God gave me a couple of years ago of you and I standing together on a stage, you testifying of how God took your sin and transformed your relationship with Him, me testifying of how God took my mess and turned it into my message, and then together, us testifying of how God brought us back together and restored our relationship to a level it would've never achieved without all the tragedies! I believe also, that your testimony will help hundreds, if not thousands, of people to avoid the same destruction in their lives.

You are not alone in this. There are already many ministers, trained by Jack Hyles, who are serving time now or have already served time in prison for molesting children. Some are their own kids, others are kids in their churches. It must stop. It affects generations for years. I believe that God has called me to be the one in our family to break the curse of incest and perversion so that my children and their children, etc., will not have to experience the insecurity, rejection, and anger, that comes with being sexually abused.

God has done a tremendously mighty work in me, and it would be an injustice to Him not to share it and bring all glory to God! I hate that the message has to include what you did to me, but that is such a small part of the overall story. The great part and biggest part is how God redeemed it and brought me into a life of gratitude for what He was able to do with me now when I felt as if I was worth nothing. There are a lot of girls out there, and boys too, that feel they aren't worth anything, so they finally decide to end their lives to stop the pain because they've never been told that they can have hope. God can get them through all the painful memories and to the other side where they can experience and live in peace and joy that cannot be explained.

Dad, I know that you know this, but I love you with all my heart. That will never change. Even though I am about to share my testimony with a group of people who worshipped you for 12 years as their pastor, I am at total peace because God has given me so many clear signs as to what He is asking me to do. This may be the final nail in the coffin of our relationship, or it may be the opening of your prison doors to finally allow you to walk in true freedom. I believe you can make a huge impact on the world with your testimony and your years of previous ministry as your training ground. However, the choice is completely yours. I pray that you choose the right one. Either way, I pray that you are blessed, and I hope that no matter what, you will never forget that I love you with all my heart forever!

Your Daughter, Wendi

The night of the Healing & Restoration Service was powerful. People didn't know what to expect from me, and I didn't know if they would run me out of the church or out of town for that matter. But, neither one happened. Though I'm sure many were confused by the revelation of what happened to me, they believed my story. Not only was I able to openly share what I went through, I invited anyone listening to me to come forward for prayer and healing. God opened the prison doors for many people that night! I never expected my crazy story to have such an impact on anyone. God's grace is very evident in my life, and without it, I would never have survived the hell I went through. A simple act of being obedient to tell my story sent my life in a direction of full-time ministry and helping others. It's a life of reward and fulfillment that I thought was completely out of reach for someone like me.

AFRICA

When the Lord has a plan for us, He sometimes does things that don't make sense to our finite minds. After my grand act of obedience, I was patiently waiting to hear the news that I was finally pregnant. I believed that I would be a mommy to a little girl because God had gone to such lengths to let me know she was coming. He also gave me explicit instructions to prepare for and anticipate her arrival. The Healing & Restoration Service was somewhat of a "distraction" from the everyday yearning of a daughter; however, my heart still longed for my baby girl.

During a visit to my brother's house a few months later, he told me of an upcoming trip he had planned to Nairobi, Kenya to visit a feeding program for orphans that lived in the slums. Brandon had been back and forth to Africa many times for his worship ministry, but I'd never gone with him. This time, I felt strongly compelled to go. I wasn't sure why because it wasn't really my thing, not to mention, it required five vaccines, and I was deathly afraid of needles at the time. Jim wasn't too excited about me going without him, but I knew that this was something God was putting on my heart. As the trip approached, we were riding in the car, and he said, "You can go to Africa with your brother if you want." I was shocked to hear the words come out of his mouth, so I immediately started to put my travel plans in motion just in case he changed his mind.

I found out later that Jim had pulled my brother aside and asked him to please not let me bring a child home. He knew I wanted a baby girl, and if we did end up adopting, he wanted the experience to be special. Having his wife bring home a daughter he would meet at the airport for the first time was not the way he planned it. My husband surely knows me.

When I got to Africa, I was overwhelmed at what I saw. There were over 700 orphans there and each of them were just needing to belong to a family. I immediately knew that I could take any of these children home with me and love them like my own. It was like God had given me a heart transplant—a new heart and a new attitude. It was the first time that I'd considered adoption. Spending time with the children was healing, and of course, I fell in love with a beautiful little girl. I wondered if her name was Jenna, it wasn't. That was okay! I thought that I could adopt her and call her Jenna! I was willing to take any and every one of these kids home if I could. They all just wanted to be loved. They were just like me! Because God gave me a major heart change about adoption, I was certain now that I could be an adoptive parent and love any of these kids that God would allow me to adopt just as I loved my own.

JENNA'S STORY

osing two babies was deeply saddening, but we knew that God would be faithful to His word and bring us the daughter that He promised. Since we had never considered adopting before, we weren't quite sure of the process. We started to put things in motion and contacted an agency to prepare ourselves in case God wanted to bring a daughter to us that way. We were told the process could take months, but it only took me about three weeks to complete the paperwork (I'm a bit of an over-achiever). Just before we got the final signature from the supervisor to approve us for adoption, I got a phone call from a friend about a couple who needed a family to adopt their baby. They thought they'd found another couple to adopt their baby but the couple they were considering were not married, and the birth parents wanted the baby to be placed in a Christian family with two married parents.

I keep learning over and over how God is on His own time schedule! We'd gone through an agency to get approved to adopt a child, but God didn't work it out that way. Once we started down the road of privately adopting, the paperwork with the potential agency adoption was put on hold (since their policies and procedures did not allow us to have two processes going at the same time.)

I got the call at the end of November. I was with my brother and his wife, Kim, in Georgia. A friend knew about a couple looking for a family for their baby. I was told the family needed to place their baby for adoption and was asked if I might be interested. I asked Kim, Brandon's wife to pray with me before I returned the call. After we prayed, I felt peace come over me, then I called my friend back. Without hesitation, I said yes. While you can't be confident about anything when it comes to adoption, I felt strongly that this was from the Lord and that we were supposed to do this. All I wanted to know was if I needed to get on a plane back to Texas that moment or if it could wait until I got home.

I was put in touch with the birth father who told me about their situation. They already had three children living with them that they struggled to take care of. I talked to him about the adoption, I was sure how he felt, but I wanted to talk to the birth mom. The birth mom called me back later that night, and we had a good conversation. We agreed to meet as soon as I returned to Tyler. Two days later, I met the birth mom for the first time at Starbucks, and we talked for three hours. It was so wonderful; we felt like we had known each other for a long time even though we had just met. She shared a couple of things with me about her story. She'd had some very sad experiences. I felt compassion because I know what it's like to have difficult things happen in life. We agreed to move forward with the adoption. The next step was to get all four of us together to talk about the adoption.

Jim and I and the birth parents met for about three hours, and we all had a lot of peace when we left that meeting. At that point, we had no idea if the baby was a boy or girl, but it was the peace in our hearts that made it clear that we were supposed to adopt the child. The birth mother had not been to the doctor but suspected she was going to be due in February or March. We set up an appointment at a local clinic for the next week to get medical care for baby and mom.

I took her to have a sonogram to find out if the baby was a girl or boy. God had made it very clear that we were supposed to adopt this baby, but what I didn't know yet was if this was the baby He promised us. The promised baby was clearly a girl. He made that blonde-proof! What if this was a boy? I had determined that no matter what, God was calling us to adopt this child. If it wasn't the child He promised, then I knew she was still in my future. But, could it be that this was the time He would fulfill His promise?

I sat on the bed with the birth mom while they looked at the baby. The nurse asked if we wanted to know what the baby was, and we both said yes. She then told us that it was a girl. A girl! This was God's promise! It was all I could do not to fall off the table from the joy and excitement I felt that moment. My legs were completely numb! I was undoubtedly overwhelmed and couldn't believe that baby Jenna was almost here. I could hardly wait as we went back and forth to various appointments. Mom and baby were progressing well, soon our baby girl would be brought into the world.

On Sunday, February 13th, I wrote this letter to her:

Dear Jenna,

I have waited so long to see this dream becoming reality, and now we are so close to seeing your beautiful face. I really thought you would be here by now, but God has a special plan in the works, and we are patiently waiting to see the whole thing unfold. You will never know the depth of love that I already have for you, and you're not even here yet! I just can't imagine what it's going to be like when I can hold you and kiss your sweet face. Your daddy and two brothers, Jace and Jaxon, are also very anxious and excited to see you. They have been praying for you for a long time. God gave me a promise almost two years ago, and now it is so close to being fulfilled. We have been anticipating and preparing for you since God gave me the first sign of the promise of you. It is truly a beautiful story, and I am so thankful for the experience God has given me. I never gave up on His promise even after having two miscarriages. God had a different plan in bringing you into our lives, and now you are almost here. I pray that I will be the best mommy in the world that I can be for you!

You will be my first daughter, and I am so excited about all the fun mother and daughter things we will be able to do together. We are finally seeing pink in this house, and it's not just in my closet! It has been so much fun shopping for all the cute stuff we got for you and your room. You also have many people waiting to meet you that love you so much. It is so hard waiting on you because I am so anxious to see and hold you. We thought you were coming last week, but it ended up being a false alarm. I know that all the waiting will be worth it in the end because we will have a lifetime together to show you just how much we love you. My prayer is that I am the best mommy you could ever have. I also pray that you will learn to love Jesus with all your heart and do mighty things for Him. Well, I am going to continue to try to be patient and wait for you to get here. I am already so in love with you, and I'm looking forward to the day when I can finally see your sweet little face!

All my love,
Mommy.

THE PROMISE FULFILLED!

Jenna Leigh was born on Friday, February 25th, at 11:17 a.m. She weighed 6 pounds 10 ounces and was 19 ½ inches long. She had dark brown hair and blue eyes and was the most beautiful baby girl I had ever seen in my life. She was absolutely perfect in every way. The doctor said she was a healthy baby. God is so good. He truly means what He says that if we delight ourselves in Him, He gives us the desires of our heart.

Psalm 37:4

Delight yourself in the Lord, and He will give you the desires of your heart. ESV

The two-year journey to Jenna started on March 11th and ended the same day two years later. It was on that day that she was ours, and no one could take her away from us.

Adopting Jenna wasn't something I had to settle for, she was more than I could have ever dreamed of. And of course, because God does exceedingly more than we can ask or think, the story didn't stop there.

My family meant more to me than I could express to anyone. I loved being a mom to my boys and little girl. The boys were the best of friends, and I wanted Jenna to have a sister, so she could have that same kind of bond.

When Jenna was about to have her first birthday, we prayed about our next steps and decided to do in vitro (IVF) to conceive our next baby. The whole time I was moving forward, I was telling the Lord that if this was not His plan to please not let it move forward. I didn't want to play God. But it seemed that all doors were open. I even got the procedure approved by my insurance, which is unheard of. God led us to an incredible Christian doctor who was amazing to work with. They didn't give me a lot of hope because of my age; I was almost 42. They told us that it usually takes a few tries before we would get pregnant. In our case, however, I was pregnant the first time around. We were very excited but decided not to tell anyone until we were sure I would be able to carry the baby to term. God had not given me any specific instructions to follow with this baby, so I kept the news to myself for a while.

The doctor was in Dallas, so we made many trips to see him to monitor the progression of the pregnancy. This time, everything was moving along well. The HCG levels were in line, and we could hear the heartbeat. After many visits to Dallas, he told us that everything was fine, and we were now released to go to our regular OB-GYN in Tyler where we lived. I couldn't have been happier. We made it. We were having a baby!

During the IVF process, the Lord had called me to do a fundraiser for the beautiful children in Africa that He had used to change my heart about adoption. Again, fundraising was something that I'd never done before, but God was asking me to be obedient and was about to reveal His faithfulness to me. He led me to do an outdoor event that seemed to be like a festival of some sort in my mind.

With absolutely no experience and no idea on how to pull it off, I announced the upcoming "No Hungry Children Benefit Festival" on Facebook (so now it was official). The event took almost six months to plan, and it was during the planning that I had my IVF procedure. Although stressful and extremely hectic, things in my life seemed to be going very well. The IVF worked on the first try, the baby was progressing, and my levels were normal, God was bringing multitudes of people together to support the fundraising effort He put on my heart; things seemed to be going very smoothly. I wasn't surprised, though, because, after all, I was being obedient, and blessings always follow obedience, right?

The time came for me to go in for a routine check up on the baby. I was so excited to hear the heartbeat again. It was so reassuring after the last two pregnancies. As the doctor prepared my belly with the cold gel for the sonogram, I listened anxiously to hear my sweet baby on the monitor. After locating the little peanut on the screen, my doctor told me that she was having trouble finding the heartbeat. I was in the middle of planning an event for the children in Africa and had faith that all would be well. After all, the Lord had given me this baby, and I was doing His work in the ministry. My faith was strong; my baby was going to be fine. I was not going to doubt that.

She was never able to locate the baby's heartbeat, but she said she was going to give me a week and then check on me again and sent me home. She told me not to be surprised if I saw blood. I didn't think much of that because I knew my baby was perfectly fine. I told everyone that the baby and I were going to be fine, and I continued to do the work in the ministry. I was giving my final presentation to a group of supporters the night before the event began when I ran to the bathroom and started bleeding. I called my doctor who met me at the clinic. I was starting to miscarry. There was no baby. It was devastating. The next day, I had to attend the festival I'd been planning for the last six months. I was raising thousands of dollars for orphans while I was losing my own baby.

I built up huge resentment toward the Lord. Nothing made sense to me. I could not understand why He would let this happen. How could He ask me to take care of the orphans when He didn't take care of my baby? Why did He even let the IVF work if I was not supposed to have this baby? Why did I have to have another miscarriage? What did I do to deserve this? I stayed in my own personal pity party for six weeks until Jim told me that I had to go away and get alone with the Lord to work through my thoughts, feelings, and questions. I didn't want to go or spend time with the Lord, but Jim didn't give me an option. Either I was going to pack for myself, or he was going to pack for me. Reluctantly, I agreed. While I was packing, I got a phone call that would change everything.

JESSA'S STORY

Jenna's birth father was calling to tell us that they had a friend who was pregnant and wanted to place her baby for adoption. She was interested in talking to us about adopting her child. It was the same situation as before. She had other children and was not able to care for another baby. Jenna's birth father told her that they had placed their baby with us, and they were happy with how things turned out and perhaps we would also adopt her baby. Then the two children would grow up together.

As I listened, I couldn't believe what I was hearing and thought it was a trick of the enemy. I thought he was kicking me while I was down. I was struggling with my faith. I took all the information and went away on my sabbatical, which was not like me at all. I normally would have jumped at the chance to meet with her, but I wasn't feeling that right at that moment. After all, who gets a second call out of the blue from someone needing a good home to place their baby for adoption?

I'd begged the Lord not to let me have another miscarriage. I was doing His work by planning a huge event for children in need when I didn't even know what I was doing. I was working for the Lord, but I didn't understand why things happened with me the way they did. Now He wanted me to believe that He was just going to give me a baby? Just like that? In my head, what happened with Jenna was a once in a lifetime thing. Now it was happening again? I wasn't falling for it. I told the Lord that He was going to have to make it crystal clear—more than He'd ever done with anything before.

On the way home from my rest, I called the birth mother. In that conversation, God started to reveal the similarities between the circumstances around Jenna's birth and this new baby's birth mom. As I listened to her talk, I was completely amazed. It was baby number six for this mom; it was baby six for Jenna's birth mother. She had already given up a child for adoption. Jenna's mom also had given up another child for adoption. She was six months pregnant when I met her, and Jenna's birth mother was six months along. The similarities kept coming. I was still skeptical but decided to cautiously move forward. Through a series of events, we ended up at the same doctor's office with the same doctor who delivered my first daughter eighteen months before. This birth mom had told me she believed this baby was a boy which would have been fine with me, although a girl seemed more ideal (in my mind) to grow up with Jenna. On our first visit to the doctor, the sonogram showed it was another baby girl. I finally believed that God was in this. The similarities were too many to ignore. Some may believe in coincidence, but with the way God had pursued me regarding Jenna, there was no question that this baby was also sent straight from Him. These similarities were exactly what I needed to let my guard down and trust that God was in this situation. The pain of losing three babies was still too raw for me to let down my guard unless I was absolutely sure that this was God's will and purpose for my life. From the day we got the call about our first daughter, Jenna, it had been ninety days until she was with us. From the day we got the call about Jessa, it was eighty-six days. We even ended up at the same hospital where Jenna was born, a hospital that we went to in the next town over because the hospital in our town sent us away when Jenna's birth mother was in labor.

God knew I was at the lowest point in my faith when Jessa came along. God was telling me that if I would just trust Him with the grain of a mustard seed, the smallest amount of faith, He would do this for me. The days I waited for Jessa were mostly good, but I did waver, wondering if it would ever happen. There was even a situation with the birth father that threatened the adoption. I remember being so devastated that it felt like I was going through another miscarriage. It was almost more than I could bear. My emotions were raw and beaten down, and they were all over the place. Even through all of that, the Lord was faithful. Jessa was born on October 1. She had blonde hair and brown eyes, just like my two boys. She was perfectly beautiful, and I was completely in love. Again! This was the prophecy fulfilled, that God would give me two baby girls.

MY GIRLS AND THEIR DAD

One of my favorite things is seeing my girls with their daddy. They will only know his love and protection. They will never go through what I went through. They will never know what it's like to be rejected by a father. They will experience the true love of a daddy, something I didn't know. I'm delighted as I watch them together.

Like the woman with the issue of blood, God saw my brokenness and had a plan for love and restoration to come into my life just like it came into her life. It was no accident that she was healed by Jesus that day. She had been looking, searching, praying and the Father saw her, healed her, and gave her a new identity.

As a mom, God has grown in me a heart for each child so that I could love the next one as much as the one before. When I die, I believe they will find four hearts in me. One for Jace, one for Jaxon, one for Jenna, and one for Jessa all wrapped in an outer layer of the love that holds us all together—Jim. My life is so blessed, and I'll never be able to repay my Heavenly Father for such a blessing of having this great family. He truly has given me more than was taken from me in my childhood family. I would go through all of it again if my blessing at the end of it was having the same family that I have now.

I never want them to forget that they are loved, and I wrote this letter to remind them:

Letter from Mom

To my Beloved, Precious Children, I am not even sure how to put into words the love I feel for each of you. There are times that I would like to be able to transmit my thoughts to allow you to read my mind and see how overwhelming the love is that I have for you. However, it has occurred to me that you may not even understand what a gift it is to experience that type of unconditional love because you have never known anything else. I wish I could say the same about my own parents.

There is nothing worse, even at almost 50 years of age, than wondering why your parents did not love you with no strings attached for no other reason besides the fact that you are their child. In fact, as a parent, I'm amazed at the amount of pain that my own parents have caused in my life. Ever since I found out that I was going to become a momma, my mission in life has been to make things completely different for each of you than it was for me.

Everything I do, everything I think, everything I strive for— it is all so that our family can be close, and you children can be secure in who you are, not just in our family, but in the eyes of Father God. Feeling a parent's rejection has been the hardest thing I have ever struggled with.

Even the sexual abuse I grew up with is nothing compared to feeling like you've been thrown out with the trash. My goal was to be sure you kids never experienced that feeling. I know I have made many mistakes as your momma; however, at the end of my life if none of you have ever wondered if or how much I love you, I will feel as though I have done a good job. This love stems only from my Parent, our heavenly Father.

Without His love for me, I could never have loved you like I have.

Love, Mom

I'm so thankful that God did not give up on me. He went to great lengths to show me His kindness and to make sure that I knew it was His love and grace working in our lives all along.

Now that the Lord had put my family in place, it was time for me to step into His call to ministry by helping others who have been through devastating situations in their lives. Unfortunately, there were more people like me out there than I ever imagined.

End Part Two
Prayer

Dear Father God,

   Please forgive me for not trusting you fully. Sometimes it seems more complicated than it really is. Help me to remember that you are just looking for me to be obedient. The results are up to you but being obedient is what I want to work on. Help me to step out in faith, even when I don't have the details, knowing You will never leave me or forsake me. Your Word promises me that You are not a man that You should lie. Life and all its circumstances can be very confusing and even frightening at times. I don't always know what to do, who to trust, or where to turn. You, however, know the answer to each of those questions and every detail surrounding it. Please help me to take my focus off my circumstances and to put my focus on You alone. Help me to trust You with the answers and for Your Holy Spirit to guide and direct me. When I make a mistake, help me to confess quickly and redirect my focus back to You instead of my mistake. The enemy is so good at keeping me wallowing in my own misery, but You promise to forgive and forget my sin so please help me to forget it and move forward as well. Thank You for always being so patient with me!

In Jesus' Name,
Amen

Scriptures:

1 Samuel 15:22

And Samuel said, "Has the Lord as great delight in burnt offerings and sacrifices, as in obeying the voice of the Lord? Behold,

*to obey is better than sacrifice, and to listen than the fat of rams.
ESV*

Hebrews 13:5-6

*Keep your life free from love of money, and be content with what
you have, for he has said, "I will never leave you nor forsake
you." So, we can confidently say, "The Lord is my helper; I will
not fear; what can man do to me?"*

Numbers 23:19

*God is not man, that he should lie, or a son of man, that he
should change his mind. Has he said, and will he not do it? Or
has he spoken, and will he not fulfill it?*

PART THREE

THE MINISTRY AND THE MESSAGE

HOPE REBUILT MY LIFE

When a girl is molested, it changes her life forever. The healing process is long, and she has a lot of questions about what happened to her. She usually feels guilt and shame and thinks she's worthless. I want young girls to know that they are loved, that they matter to the Lord and to others. With this in my heart, God showed me that it was time to step out and tell my story. He showed me that, in the telling of my story and what happened with my father, other people would experience freedom.

I asked Him for confirmation before I took one step into ministry. I knew that if God told me to do it, then He would be with me no matter what happened. Just as before, He gave me the confirmation I needed.

I was apprehensive at first, but God confirmed His instructions to me that led me to go back to my childhood church and give my testimony. When my dad left the church all those years ago a lot of people were hurt and left to wonder what happened. I didn't know what to expect when I told them the truth. Would they throw tomatoes at me and run me off the stage? Would they even believe me? God in His grace allowed me to have my pastor there who had met with my dad and me before, knew the whole story and had confirmed the details. He was ready to speak on my behalf if anyone had anything to say or felt I wasn't telling the truth. Thankfully, it wasn't necessary for him to speak for me, because the people believed me. I went on to speak at several other churches and women's ministries, telling my story, praying for women, and watching God heal and set them free. God was using my simple obedience to heal the hearts of so many others. The purpose in the pain was finally starting to make sense to me.

Sadly, the connection with my dad has not yet been restored even though I pray that it will be restored one day. My kids and my brother's kids lost a Pawpaw, and my dad is missing out on knowing our beautiful and amazing children.

FORGIVEN

Forgiveness came easy for me with my dad. I have forgiven him and have so much love for him in my heart. I pray that one day our relationship is healed and restored. After all that I've been through, it may be strange for you to read that I forgive my dad, but it's true. My dad, and men like him, are like the woman with the issue of blood. They have a condition that's steeped in distortion and brokenness and disrupts normal life. There is shame, fear, hiding, lying, and hurt in that brokenness. Whether they know it or not, they too need a touch from Christ. They are typically alone in their condition. Many child abusers were themselves abused by someone, most of them never told a soul. Instead of reaching out for Christ, they kept it inside and tried to handle it their own way. Molesters keep secrets for many reasons, some of which include their own fear of being an outcast or being publicly shamed. I would only be telling half of the story if I didn't reach out to tell my dad and men like him that God's love is strong enough to forgive and heal them.

1 John 1:9

If we confess our sins, He is faithful and just and will forgive our sins and purify us from all unrighteousness. ESV

This is important for the offender and the people around them. If someone in your life comes to you for help, please don't attack them. You can be sure that if they are reaching out, they know they need help. This is true for any person with any struggle. It could be molestation, adultery, pornography, dancing, stealing, abortion, or things we have never thought of. There are times when people need help to get free, and they often turn to those they feel they can be open and honest with. God's love can reach us all.

It would be no different for an abuser than it was for the woman with the issue of blood or than it was for me. If, in an act of faith, he was desperate and reached out to touch Jesus, Jesus would have compassion and healing for that man. His act of faith would lead to healing just as it did in the woman, but something more important than healing would happen for the abuser. Jesus would acknowledge a repentant abuser and claim him for His own. Just as the woman became His daughter, a repentant man becomes a forgiven son.

I completely understand how someone could hate a child molester and I would be justified to hate them too. But, when I think of the grace that God has for all mankind, I can't help but think of how much Jesus wants to heal them. It's not that I don't struggle with the thought of forgiving an abuser, I completely forgive my dad, but I still struggle to forgive others who hurt me. It's a real battle for me sometimes, and I can only depend on the Lord to keep me from living in the unforgiveness.

After bleeding for twelve years and being an outcast, who did the woman have to talk to about her illness? It's the same with men who abuse physically, sexually, emotionally, or spiritually. They know something is wrong, but who can they trust or turn to that will not judge them? Not only do they deceive others, but they also deceive themselves. That deception can fool everyone, but it can't fool God. God wants to heal all brokenness in us.

If you have hurt or abused another person in any way, God has a way out for you. He knows your distress and feels the pain and shame that you live with. He wants to heal you, bring you peace, and put your heart in order. He wants to give you a real life that you can be proud of. Don't try alone anymore; reach out to someone who can help you. There are ministries and organizations who understand and will help you.

At one point in my life, it seemed like my hopes and dreams were shattered. I didn't know that God had a plan of restoration for every single dream that I had. He was making things right even when I didn't know He was working on my behalf. In fact, He was making a way for me even before I cried out to Him for help. I saw a saying on Facebook from Philip Yancey that said, "Jesus forgave a thief dangling on a cross, knowing full well the thief had converted out of plain fear. That thief would never study the Bible, never attend synagogue or church, and never make amends to those he had wronged. He simply said, 'Jesus, remember me,' and Jesus promised, 'Today, you will be with me in paradise.' It was another shocking reminder that grace does not depend on what we have done for God, but rather what God has done for us."

Salvation is a gift from God that we could never earn, but for me, it's the amazing grace behind the gift of salvation and everything that it cost Jesus to make it possible for me, that drives me to want to please my Heavenly Father. If He can forgive me for all that I've done that caused the death of His Son, how can I not forgive others who have hurt me? We are forgiven by God and He asks that we forgive others. Forgiveness does not mean that what they did to us was okay or that we allow an abuser to keep hurting us, it means we have compassion on another soul just as God the Father has compassion on us. Forgiveness is the only tool that allows us to move forward without bitterness and resentment. Those things do nothing but hurt us, and personally, I would rather walk in the freedom God provided for me at the cross. You may have heard this before, but unforgiveness is like drinking poison and hoping the other person dies. Forgiveness is for you and me and never condones what happened to us. It is just a choice to cut the shackles that keep us chained to our offenders. It also doesn't mean that you must reconcile with your offender. Although I am a strong advocate of reconciliation, I believe there are cases, like mine, where the relationship with the offender is toxic and that letting them go is the best thing to do. God is bigger than any situation we face, and if we will turn to Him for help instead of choosing to wallow in our pain, He can heal and repair our hearts and draw us close to Him. That is the safest place to be. In time, His plan and purpose for the pain will be revealed, but until then, we can trust Him to work all things for our good and His glory.

Colossians 1:13-14

[13] He has delivered us from the domain of darkness and trans-ferred us to the kingdom of his beloved Son, [14] in whom we have redemption, the forgiveness of sins. ESV

UNQUALIFIED CALLING

We learned a lot when we adopted our daughters. It was not as expensive as other adoptions that we'd heard about nor was it as difficult. God called us to help other couples adopt children. He also led us to start a home for unwed pregnant young girls that would help them either parent or place their babies for adoption.

With faith in God and without any special qualifications, we started Chosen One Adoption Agency, an organization that helps couples adopt children in a respectful and affordable way and The Magdalene Home, a place for young pregnant girls to receive care while they carry their babies and either parent them or place them for adoption. I knew nothing about starting a non-profit organization, but I had faith in God. I knew that the God of hope was still doing miracles today. Hope is powerful when you embrace it and let it sink down deep in your soul.

Scholar and Pastor John Piper writes:

"Biblical hope is not a mere desire for something good to happen. It is a confident expectation and desire for something good in the future. Biblical hope has moral certainty in it. When the Word says, "Hope in God!" it does not mean, "Cross your fingers." It means, to use the words of William Carey, 'Expect great things from God."

When difficult things happen, we are invited by God to have a strong hope that He is working everything together for our good and for His glory. Difficulties and hardship look different when they are seen through the eyes of love and hope. This does not discount the hurt and pain of the hard things that happen in life; it means that those things don't have to destroy or define you.

Romans 8:28

And we know that for those who love God all things work together for good,[a] for those who are called according to his purpose.

That means that there is not one thing that God won't work together for our good because we love Him (and He loves us) and we are called for *His* purpose.

God's love is pure and real, not like any love that you have ever encountered. It is safe and expects nothing in return. When abuse or abandonment happens, it can hurt to the core and make you doubt that anyone, including God, loves you.

You're not alone if you have had the feelings of not being sure if God's love was for you or if you have doubt and insecurity after suffering hard times. Every person who has ever been deeply hurt has this experience. Sometimes those feelings quickly melt once they are covered with the blood of Jesus and, at other times, healing is progressive. It's like the men in the Bible who were healed by Jesus—*as they went.*

Luke 17 11-19

On the way to Jerusalem he was passing along between Samaria and Galilee.[12] And as he entered a village, he was met by ten lepers,[f] who stood at a distance[13] and lifted up their voices, saying, "Jesus, Master, have mercy on us." When he saw them he said to them, "Go and show yourselves to the priests." And as they went they were cleansed. [15] Then one of them, when he saw that he was healed, turned back, praising God with a loud voice; [16] and he fell on his face at Jesus' feet, giving him thanks. Now he was a Samaritan. Then Jesus answered, "Were not ten cleansed? Where are the nine? Was no one found to return and give praise to God except this foreigner?" And he said to him, "Rise and go your way; your faith has made you well."^{ESV}

As they were walking in obedience, faith, and hope in Jesus, their healing began to manifest. The same can be true for you. You may have prayed and prayed to be healed or to have a certain hurt taken away. Be encouraged and keep walking. Ask God to show you what to do. It is the walking in obedience, faith, and hope that brings on greater and greater levels of healing.

The fact that I have faith comes from the Lord and reading His Word. I believe that every good gift comes from the Father. Those who know me know that even though I have faith I also like to have a plan and I like those plans to work out right. But there is a dichotomy between faith and having a plan. It's good if I know what's in front of me and what's going to happen next. But If I knew everything that was going to happen I wouldn't need faith. I wouldn't need to put one foot in front of the other and trust God. It's walking by faith that puts motion to the work we do with young girls and families. *"Rise and go your way; your faith has made you well."* The lepers were healed by Jesus, but they had to walk by faith and go do what He told them to do (obedience) to experience the miracle. My team and I experience miracles as we go and do what He has told us to do. I had no idea how to start an adoption agency, but I knew God would not tell me to do something unless He was going to make it possible. A part of having faith is doing what you're called to do even when you can't see the way clearly. The Bible tells us in Hebrews that without faith, it is impossible to please God. Despite every circumstance, obeying God matters more than anything. Even when I think I can't do something, He gives me the strength to do what at first looks impossible.

THE FIRST BABY

The first baby adopted through Chosen One Adoption Agency was baby Williams, a little girl. She became the daughter of parents who had hoped and prayed for her even before she was born. Their hearts were filled with love for her.

They had tried to conceive for two and a half years with no idea that a physical problem would keep them from having their own children. For five years they prayed, waited, went through treatments and then embraced the idea of adoption. They struggled to trust God and hold on to hope when things around them looked hopeless. Other couples were having children while they kept trying without success. After several miscarriages, they still had the deep desire to be parents but realized that God may grant them children in a different way. They became open to adoption. They registered with an adoption agency in Georgia where they lived. After two years on a waiting list, they still had not been chosen by a birth mother. The hope and anticipation they once felt turned to sadness. On the outside, they tried to stay positive and put on the happy face. On the inside, they were hurting and fighting off disappointment. Going to church and serving in the nursery became harder and harder. Their hearts were full of love for a child they didn't have yet.

They didn't know that across the country there was a family of four living in a hotel and expecting another child. They were good parents who struggled to take care of the children they had. In fact, if they kept this third child, Child Protective Services would take all three children deeming the parents unfit because of the lack of resources to care of their children.

Right after we got the agency up and running, I received a call from the birth mother. She didn't need a place to stay so she was not going to be a part of The Magdalene Home. She asked me many questions about adoption and how the process worked. When I found out that they could barely take care of the two children they had, and if they kept this one, all their children would be taken away from them, I wanted to help. They chose to place their baby for adoption with us.

They wanted the baby to be adopted by a Godly family and knew that we were placing children in Christian homes. A few weeks later I was in Georgia visiting my brother. He knew a couple who had been trying for a very long time to have a child and were now working with a local adoption agency. They had been waiting a long time but with no luck. Our agency was in Texas, but my brother still wondered if we could help them. I called my administrator and asked if we could help them even though they didn't live in Texas. As it turned out, as long as the baby was in Texas, we could help them. I called the adoptive parents to see if they were interested, and they absolutely wanted consideration to be parents of this little girl. They were one of five other families who signed up to work with us at our first orientation. There is a process that each couple must go through with our agency to be presented to the birth families, and then they find out if they have been chosen by the birth family to adopt their baby.

After waiting and praying for what seemed like an eternity, it was their turn. They were chosen by the birth family. I had to do a little detective work to find the new parents and let them know. When I did, they were at a birthday dinner for my brother. I told them the good news over a speaker phone with a room full of people who were excited to celebrate with them. At first, it looked like God was not answering their prayers, but all the while He was setting things up in the background.

The birth parents loved their baby, but the serious circumstances didn't allow them to keep her. There are many reasons that children are placed with new parents for adoption and it's not always for the reasons we think. This mom and dad had a difficult choice to make. It was from a pure heart of love that they placed their baby girl in the care of another couple. Think about it for a moment. That little baby had a double portion of love as she came into the world.

Seeing the adoption come together was like watching the pieces of a giant puzzle from heaven fit perfectly to reveal a beautiful image. Circumstances and connections, chance meetings and the impeccable timing of events all happened so that this baby could be introduced to her new family and her new life.

It was like God was moving heaven and earth so that these families could receive the miracle that He had planned for them. I've seen the Lord move heaven and earth many times for those who love Him and for those who are yet to know Him. His care is so deep that even when we are not aware that He is orchestrating His mercy around us, it is happening anyway.

I can relate to that little child. I was in need, with no place to turn. God chose to redeem me and fill me with His love and grace. My life was on the brink of destruction and uncertainty. He adopted me, and He loved me.

Before we are born, God knows us. Before hurt or tragedy happens, God creates a plan for healing and redemption. He doesn't wait until we get it together or figure it all out. God, like the parents of that little baby, is prepared to take us as we are and love us so deeply that we cannot deny that we belong to Him.

Psalm 110:3 reminds us that we belong to God. The Common English Bible states: *"Know that the Lord is God-He made us; we belong to Him."* The Hebrew text literally means "we are His."

Nothing can ever change that.

Knowing where you belong is like an anchor that keeps you from blowing in the wind. It holds you down and connects you to God and others. God wants us to know that He not only made us, but He deeply loves us; we belong to Him.

THE BANQUET

Each year there is a banquet for The Magdalene Home. It's attended by the girls who live there, the people who support the ministry and those who want to know more about what we're doing. During the banquet, the vision and progress of the home are shared with supporters and the community. Area leaders, local churches, and non-profits attend as well as those who give their time, money and professional resources to make it all happen. Some of the supporters can relate to the girls because they have been where they are now. Others become supporters because they know we are changing lives. Not just the lives of the girls, we are changing lives of their children. The impact is felt by two generations at a time. The focus of the event is on the home, the girls, and on sharing the compassion of Jesus.

At one of our last banquets, my Board thought it would be a good idea for my brother to introduce me since he has been walking this journey with me all my life. Rather than tell you what he said, I've included his words here:

"When I was first asked if I was willing to introduce my sister tonight, I immediately said, "Of course, I'd be happy to. It'd be a pleasure and a privilege," and then I hung up and started pan-icking thinking, "What am I going to say that's not going to get

me and/or her in trouble?" You see, one of the things I love about my sister is we're a lot alike. I'm not sure what that says about me.

She's one of my favorite people on the planet. We're a lot alike, but, or maybe, I'm a lot like her, right? She came first. I think I understand her more than anybody on the planet. In fact, she says that we were twins, and I'm just a little slow and came out two-and-a-half years later.

We both tell it like it is. We both like to be in charge. You don't know me, but you're saying, yes, yes, yes about Wendi right now. We're both stubborn. That's because we're both always right. You can just ask our spouses.

We both move very quickly because we're trying to get stuff done, but sometimes we run over people that are in front of us that are moving a little too slow, but we will always stop and help them up.

We both have to ask forgiveness a lot, but we're both quick to forgive. We both love deeply because we know those who are forgiven much love much. We both are extremely sensitive. We both wear our feelings on our sleeves, neither one of us have any kind of poker face whatsoever. You know exactly what we're thinking and if we're happy with you at the moment.

But as much as we're alike and I promise that I'm not going to cry. As much as we are alike, we are different in a lot of ways.

To state the obvious, I'm not a woman, never have been, never will be, just making sure everybody's on the same page with me!

I've never been a mom. I've never been a wife. I've never given birth. I've never been a daughter. Never been molested by my father. I've never been raped. I've never been thrown out of my home and abandoned as a 14-year old, never had to use my body to make money. I've never resolved to kill myself. I've never had a miscarriage or three miscarriages, for that matter.

I've never had a ministry to abused girls. I've never adopted a child let alone two children within nineteen months of each other. I've never started a crisis pregnancy home or an adoption agency. I've never had a heart like my sister for the pregnant woman or the young girl who finds herself asking the tough question about keeping or ending the life of a baby.

A few years ago, I was sitting down with my pastor talking to him about what God was doing in my heart with No Hungry

Children, the organization I started, and he said something I will never forget. He said, "Brandon, you were made for this. You were made for this." As I think about what God is doing in The Magdalene Home and Chosen One Adoption Agency, I can't help but to think about my sister and how she was made for this. This is what she's put on this planet for.

I believe that God has allowed her to go through incredible pain and loss and experience abandonment and hopelessness, so He could save her and give her new life, and adopt her into His family, and give her a hope that endures forever. Now, with the help of many of you in this room, the hope of Christ is being passed on to young girls, their unborn babies, and adoptive parents. The best news is I think that God is just getting started!

Without further ado, it is my distinct pleasure to introduce the founder of The Magdalene Home and Chosen One Adoption Agency, my sister, one of my best friends, and one of my heroes, Wendi Rees."

All my life, I wanted to know what it was like to be loved and adored by my father. What I have learned over the years is there is nothing like the love of our Heavenly Father. We don't have to earn His love; we only need to receive it.

It has been a journey, but I ended up exactly where I am supposed to be.

God turned my mourning to joy, my ashes into beauty and my sorrow into hope. As my friend Chris says, *He's a God who turns orphans into daughters.*

What He did for me, He will do for you!

A PERSONAL MESSAGE

I desperately wish I could have known the truth about me when I was younger. I felt worthless, hopeless, broken, and ugly. I felt as though no one would ever want me. The shame I lived with had become a prison in my heart with walls so thick that no one could get close enough to penetrate it. More importantly, I could not get out. I was shackled to my shame. A prisoner to my pain—freedom seemed like an unattainable dream.

It wasn't until I realized that God required nothing of me, but He loved me, accepted me, and gave His life for me. I just needed to believe in Him.

Trusting was very difficult for me. Having been hurt by the one person put in my life to protect me, trusting anyone was not even an option. However, in time God proved Himself faithful to me. He started showing me in little ways at first, how to trust Him. From learning to trust Him in the little things, I learned to trust Him in bigger things.

He always meets us right where we are. He does not require us to get "cleaned up" before He loves us. Remember Rahab, the active, working prostitute that God used to help the spies? He saved her and her whole family because she simply trusted Him while she was living in blatant sin.

Please believe me when I tell you this "trusting" is a process, just like forgiveness is a process. You start out with baby steps and move one step at a time. Babies fall on their faces a lot when they first start to walk. With a little consistency, they get better and before you know it they are running around everywhere. It's the same with learning to trust God, our perfect Father, who will never leave or forsake us.

Psalm 27:10 promises us, "Though my father and mother forsake me, the LORD will receive me." Please listen to me and save yourself the years of pain that I wish I could have avoided. God is a faithful and good Father! He is a good Daddy. His love is a pure love with no strings attached. It took me a while to really learn this.

I failed many times and waited for the "hammer" to fall. Instead, each time I saw His arms of grace reach down to pick me up. I finally realized the truth. God loves me no matter what—not because of how good I am, but because of how great He is. He sees us as He sees Jesus because of Jesus' blood. And, hold on to your seat—He loves us just the same as He loves Jesus! What? Is that true? Yes, it is! My very favorite verse in the Bible is John 17:23; Jesus is praying to the Father right before He goes to the cross. Jesus asks the Father to help us know that He sent Him, and that God the Father loves us like He loves Jesus! I love the Amplified Version (AMP), "I in them and You in Me, that they may be perfected and completed into one, so that the world may know [without any doubt] that You sent Me, and [that You] have loved them, just as You have loved Me."

It took some time to grasp what Jesus prayed. I completely understand how God loves Jesus, He's perfect! But, loving me is a different story. The Bible says that He loves me the same as He loves Jesus. I had a choice to make. I could either call God a liar, which I'm not willing to do, or I could believe His promises. I say yes to His promises. If only I had known how valuable, beautiful, worthy, and accepted I really was to the only One that matters, I could have avoided many poor choices that I made. I made those choices because I was trying to find that value in other things.

I want you to know that you are not reading this book by chance. God is actively pursuing you and wants you to know His love for you. His love for you is strong, all you have to do is receive it. Will you please open your heart, even if just a little, and allow Him to lavish you with His perfect love for you? He loves you, and He is waiting.

If you don't know Jesus, He is waiting to meet you. John 3:16 and 17 says that God loved the world (you) so very much that He gave us His Son, Jesus. Whoever believes in Him shall not perish but have eternal life. For God did not send His Son into the world to condemn the world, but to save the world through Him.

John 3:16–17

"For God so loved the world,[a] that He gave His only Son, that whoever believes in Him should not perish but have eternal life. [17] For God did not send His Son into the world to condemn the world, but in order that the world might be saved through Him. ESV

If you would like to contact us:
CaptivatedByGrace.com
Wendi@CaptivatedByGrace.com
TheMagadaleneHome.com
Wendi@TheMagadaleneHome.com

APPENDIX A

WHAT IS AN INDEPENDENT FUNDAMENTAL BAPTIST CHURCH?

The word "Independent" means that the church is not a member of any council, convention or is a part of any hierarchy outside the local congregation. An Independent Baptist Church would not be a part of a national organization that would exercise authority over the local church. Thus, the name "independent" means that the church patterns itself after the New Testament example and stands alone under the authority of the Bible. Independent churches have no organized organization over them in authority. For more information, please see: BaptistDeception.com

APPENDIX B

There were a lot of rules to follow in our church. In fact, if you did any kind of work in the church, you had to sign the following agreement:

QUALIFICATIONS FOR KEY WORKERS

- Unless providentially hindered, be in attendance, and on time, for all services of the church. Sunday school, Sunday morning, and Sunday evening, Wednesday Bible study, Revival services, and all other special meetings of the church or those related to my particular job.

- Support the pastor and programs of the church with 100% loyalty and total cooperation.

- Perform my duties to the best of my ability, realizing this is God's business, not my own.

- Abstain from all worldly practices and habits not in keeping with Word of God and the standards of this church. The following should be avoided: use of any form of alcoholic beverages, use of tobacco in any form. Hollywood movies, dancing, playing cards, mixed swimming. Dresses of modest length (dresses are to be at least to the top of the knee) the wearing of slacks or shorts by women, the wearing of long hair by men on the ear or over the collar. Listening to rock music (hard or soft) reading magazines with immoral, immodest or suggestive pictures or articles, watching questionable television programs and/or any other practice which could hurt the testimony of the church or the cause of Christ.

- Support the church with at least 10% of my income.

- Participate in the visitation program of the church or at least spend two hours each week in personal and soul winning visitation.

Relinquish my position of leadership if it ever becomes impossible for me to agree with and or abide by the above.

APPENDIX C

The National Association of Christian Recovery describes Spiritual Abuse this way:

There are several ways in which abuse can be *spiritual* abuse. People use this term with a variety of meanings and it is quite important to keep track of which definition people have in mind.

There is a sense in which all abuse can be *spiritual* abuse. For example, any form of child abuse can do damage to a child's emerging spirituality. The fact that the damage includes damage to the spiritual self is what makes it *spiritual* abuse in addition to whatever other kind of abuse is going on.

Some abuse is *spiritual* abuse because it takes place in a spiritual place/context. Sexual abuse by a priest or pastor, for example, is clearly a form of spiritual abuse in addition to sexual abuse.

The use of spiritual truths or biblical texts to do harm is another form of *spiritual* abuse. Sometimes battered wives are told that God wants them to be submissive to their husbands. Sometimes children who are being molested by their parents are told that God wants them to be obedient. Sometimes people quote "do not think of yourself more highly that you ought" to suicidal or depressed people. These are examples of abuse—even if what is said is a quote from the Bible, even if 'submission' and 'obedience' are in a general sense virtues. It is the twisting of good things to do harm, that is so disturbing about this kind of abuse.

Some abuse is *spiritual* abuse because the *victim* is perceived to be in a position of spiritual authority. Think here, for example, of the abuse of pastors by congregations. The real power in religious systems may not be in the hands of the obvious leadership.

Coercive spirituality is a form of spiritual abuse. This is most obvious in totalitarian cults. But there are many other forms of coercion. Compulsive religious practices are thought by some to be appropriate forms of Christian education of children. Others more committed to the notions of 'soul freedom' and 'liberty of conscience' are repelled at the idea of religious coercion.

Some abuse is *spiritual* abuse because it invokes divine authority to manipulate people into performing behaviors which meet the needs of the abuser. Example: If I am anxious in my relationship with God and I think that 'success' in evangelistic activities will solve that problem, then I may try to get someone to convert so that I will feel less anxious. This 'using' of someone else's spiritual life to meet my spiritual needs is uncomfortably analogous to someone who 'uses' another person's sexuality to meet their own needs. The latter is sexual abuse. The former is spiritual abuse.

Some abuse is *spiritual* abuse because it introduces a grace-less contingency in our relationship with God.

119

APPENDIX D

10 Toxic Stages of Performance-Based Christianity–Are You Stuck in the Performance Hamster Wheel? By Mark DeJesus

Getting free of performance-based Christianity will revolutionize your life, but I have found that many people need to untangle themselves from the cycle that this kind of living produces. Unfortunately, the toxic thread of performance has woven itself into almost every fabric of people's lives.

Getting free is possible and life changing, but it takes intentional recognition and desire to change, otherwise the performer will get locked into a never ending "Performance Hamster Wheel."

Here are the ten stages of this performance-based Christianity that has become a counterfeit in so many lives.

STAGE 1: A LACK OF LOVE AND IDENTITY EXISTS

You were meant to be loved and affirmed in who you are and not just for what you do. Performance-based Christianity exists in people who have not experience identity affirmation. Therefore, they feel they need to perform well to feel loved by God and people around them.

Instead of having an identity as a son who is loved by our Father in heaven, performers live as spiritual slaves, where their identity is based on what they do and how well they do it.

They evaluate their relationship with God based on how well they perform religious duties and maintain a level of righteous works.

Spiritual sons know they are loved by God for who they are, not just for what they do. Slaves have no sense of affirmation apart from their works.

Sonship involves knowing you are loved by God for who you are, not just for what you do.

When that void of identity is not filled, a broken heart is trained to perform for attention, approval and validation. They see earning love through performance as the only option.

STAGE 2: COUNTERFEIT MINDSETS ENTER

When you're not secure in who you are, performance brings in some easy lures to grab onto. It entices spiritual slaves with dreams of success, status and achievement, while slowly draining the person of love, satisfaction and peace.

Performance-based living is an easy temptation for spiritual slaves.

Law Based Thinking

One of the spiritual errors that reinforces performance-based Christianity is "law-based thinking." You will see the Scriptures as a rulebook rather than an invitation for relationship. Law-based thinking reinforces performers, where they keep an evaluation of themselves based on how well they are keeping up with good works. On days you perform well, it seems that God is "OK" with you. On days you don't, He seems silent, distant and disappointed.

Thoughts scream to "work harder" and "do more," to try to get into a better place with God. This all keeps a person from experiencing the unconditional love and acceptance from God. When works override being loved unconditionally, God's design for life becomes spoiled.

At this stage, the problem is that toxic thinking has infected the motives of a person. They are now unknowingly chasing after love and performing for it all along the way. Most of the time, they are not even aware of this motivation. They just feel a "drive" or "impulse" propelling them into their daily actions.

Fabricated Personas

Performance-based Christianity promotes that believers develop fabricated personas, where they don't know how to be themselves in their ministry and Christian interaction. Performance-based Christianity conditions us to think that we are more "anointed" when we get into a certain "persona." Many pastors don't know how to just be themselves and let who they are flow authentically.

Too many people don't know to just be themselves.

I tell people all the time: be yourself as you are learning who you are each day. Today more than ever, we need dynamic and authentic communication from people being themselves, not a fabrication. For decades, Performance-based Christianity has taught us that putting on a "show" is the most effective way to change lives. When in reality, authentic living, with healthy vulnerability is where leaders can invite people into the same journey they are in themselves.

The most anointed you can be is yourself.

Toxic Belief Systems of Performance-Based Christianity

Throughout this stage, rejection is subtly implanting counterfeit values. If you're honest with yourself, you may find these rejection-based motives lurking within.

Here are toxic beliefs that performers carry deep down. Performers:

- Feel they have to earn the love and acceptance of others.

- Base how they feel about themselves on how well they perform their daily duties. "If I don't do well, I will not be loved."

- Spend a lot of time mulling over the worries or pressures of tomorrow and fear not doing well in whatever they do. "I will not be accepted or belong."

- Tend to strive and live in a "works" mentality.

- Live from pressure, where situations fall back on their efforts.

- Do things to get a sense of God's approval.

- Take themselves and what they do too seriously.

- Overthink how they come across to others.

- Have this excessive need to be "successful" and become known for their accomplishments.

- Are not comfortable with vulnerability and weakness.

- Often ignore important relational and identity issues of the heart, usually just to keep going and moving. Remember, with performance, the "show must go on."

Performers do things to get approval. Secure people know God already approves them.

STAGE 3: PERFORMANCE-BASED LIVING BECOMES A WAY OF LIFE

If no one paid attention to our performance, then this subject would not even be an issue. The problem is our culture feeds performance in every way. We spend more time affirming what people do than loving who people are unconditionally.

Performers get affirmation for what they do. It becomes an instant hit that brings them momentary pleasure. They feel good receiving it, but the affirming lands in a bucket that has holes in it. Affirmation is needed over and over. Performers live off the affirmation they get from doing, to the point that it dictates their life.

Performance-based people suck in affirmation like a vacuum, but then quickly return for more. They find that performance is the only way to experience any sense of affirmation, so they invest more energy into becoming better at whatever they do. Their work and activities become their primary source of identity.

STAGE 4: PERFORMANCE-BASED LIVING KICKS BACK

Over the long haul, performance-based living wears a person out. Toxic behaviors begin to manifest in such a way that relationships are hindered, wholeness begins to collapse and health starts to wane.

There are many performance "backlashes" that become evident over time, including when a person:

- Comes across as always busy, overloaded and overworked.

- Manifests a deep "need to succeed" at all costs, so the performer becomes immersed in activity.

- Become a workaholic with driven and perfectionistic tendencies.

- Have a "win/lose" attitude about life and issues.

- Becomes argumentative and overly competitive.

- Feels the need to be the "grown up one" in the room.

- Struggles with being a false burden bearer.

- Gives out love but cannot receive it.

- Helps others but is uncomfortable with receiving help. Ministers to others but does not present as someone who can be ministered to. Cannot receive something from someone without feeling the need to have to do something back.

- Does not know how to be themselves and just "be" in relationships.

- Struggle with relational intimacy, so they just stay busy.

- Complains of loneliness. They have spent so much time performing, that investments in their relationships have not been a priority.

- Battles with anger, either pent up or expressed.

- Carries deep fabrications that work well in the performance setting but fall apart in normal relationship interactions.

The performer is often not aware as to why these toxic fruits are manifesting, so they just dive deeper into busyness of performing and avoid pausing to deal with their inner brokenness. They often think that this is just the way life is, so these patterns become deeply embedded.

STAGE 5: A LACK OF FULFILLMENT MANIFESTS

Even though the performer's life may be busy, filled with activity and accomplishments, there is still an emptiness that remains at the end of the day. Performers feel lonely and unfulfilled when it comes to love, yet they have no idea how to get off the hamster wheel. They are starving, in desperate need of love, but they just keep going.

The lack of fulfillment is present because they have never been affirmed in love apart from what they do. Sonship is foreign because all they have known is slavery. The emptiness needs to be filled with relational connection, but performers don't have time to go deeper in relationship.

STAGE 6: ADDICTIONS ENTER

In the absence of unconditional love and acceptance in the performer's heart, they will turn to anything in search of fulfillment. Their daily grind of doing, going and performing leaves huge voids that are never satisfied.

In the absence of unconditional love, people will perform for love.

At the end of the day, when the curtain falls, people left the building and the performer is alone, darkness and loneliness creeps in. In this setting addictions rise to the occasion. Food addictions and pornography are the most common, but they can certainly manifest in any habit, behavior or pattern that cannot be broken with an act of the will. Workaholism is often a partner to other addictions.

Many do not realize that addiction struggles of any kind are often rooted in performance-orientated living. When you live in performance mode, there is little room left for dealing with the brokenness and wounds that are demanding us to tend to them.

Addictions offer a false, quick relief. They find a way to keep the person locked in a secret prison. The person hates them but attempts to get free through more performance-oriented self-help steps, while missing the root problem of a broken heart.

STAGE 7: SHAME AND GUILT ARE FELT

The person is unfulfilled and bound to vices that won't budge. Deep down, the performer feels like a fraud or a hypocrite. The guilt over their addictions creates a shame that covers them like a shroud.

Satan has a field day in their thoughts, accusing them in every way possible. The world around them can even be ignorant to the war occurring inside the performer who carries a sense of unworthiness and even uncleanness before God yet keeps the outside facade intact.

STAGE 8: MORE PERFORMANCE IS ENGAGED

The biggest problem is that the performer does not know how to get free from this vicious cycle. So, they do the only thing they have been trained to do well, perform more. Performance-based Christianity teaches us to do more good things in order to feel better about ourselves. So, they add extra effort, pushing with greater force and self-effort to achieve fulfillment through more activity.

In the church, this is where hyper-religious activity increases, thus reinforcing Performance-based Christianity. People think if they serve more, it will make them feel better about themselves before God. The problem is churches love Performance-based people, because they get more things done. Yet they often sacrifice the life of their heart on the altar of doing.

STAGE 9: THE CRASH

The performer's resources wane and they eventually crash emotionally. They have lived in the hamster wheel of performance for too long and their body screams for relief. Up until this point, the toxic roots of brokenness have been ignored, but now they are flailing. This is usually where phrases like "burnout" and "I am exhausted" become common expressions.

Most of the people who come to me for help are at this stage of the hamster wheel. They did not see the need for help before, especially because they believed the myth that performance living was working for them. Additionally, most of the time, performance people who crash want a quick fix, because that is how they live their life. "Give me a pill, say a quick prayer, do what you need to do to get me back out there." But it doesn't work like that.

STAGE 10: BACK TO PERFORMANCE

This is, actually, the saddest part of this cycle. Instead of getting some heart-help and restoration, the performer stands up from a burned-out crash and gets right back on the wheel. At the crash, the performer was halted, overwhelmed and in crisis.

They often stop everything to bring attention to their cracked emotional state. But performers are not comfortable with stillness and inactivity, so as soon as they feel a little energy return, they get right back into the race, without taking the time to heal and make necessary changes.

The cycle repeats itself and over time, relationships are depleted. The performer loses touch with friends, and family becomes an unfulfilling place of hidden resentment. It takes great courage and humility for this performance trap to be confronted and eradicated.

The only way to break free from this cycle is to recognize it, fill the foundation of your heart with God's approval and create a new pattern of living, where you don't perform for love. You live out of the love that God already has for you. (Used by permission)

BIBLIOGRAPHY

You Belong to God Daily Reflections/Produced by the High Call

Academic Journal of Interdisciplinary Studies Vol 4 No 1 MCSER Publishing, Rome-Italy March 2015 Father and Daughter Relationship and Its Impact on Daughter's Self-Esteem and Academic Achievement Asbah Zia

John Piper, Desiring God, Hope in God (DesiringGod.com)

BaptistDeception.com

Establishing a Kingdom Culture, Part 1: Identify, the key to transformation. Aglow International, Graham Cooke

www.ingramcontent.com/pod-product-compliance
Lightning Source LLC
Chambersburg PA
CBHW060502280326
41933CB00014B/2834